Greenhouse Gardening for Fun

1. A small lean-to greenhouse furnishes a **wealth** of flowers in early spring.
(ROCHE PHOTO)

Greenhouse Gardening for Fun

by Claire L. Blake

M. Barrows & Company, Inc.
Distributed by William Morrow & Co., Inc.
New York

To Helen Van Pelt Wilson
for her confidence,
encouragement and inspiration

Contents

By Way of Thanks

A "green thumb" is a great asset, and it can be acquired, although I think I inherited mine from my Grandfather Philip. Anyway, working with plants has delighted me since childhood, but for years I longed for a greenhouse where the bleak winter months could be as flower-filled as the sunny days of summer. When my dream became a reality, I talked a lot about my exciting new greenhouse. I discovered then that my friends were inclined to consider the whole thing a tremendous amount of hard work. Although many of them enjoyed out-door gardening, they could not understand my enthusiasm for twelve months of growing. They thought I exaggerated when I insisted that little time and effort were required to produce, for instance, my marvelous cattleya orchids.

Hence this book. If it convinces you who read it that greenhouse gardening can be more fun than work, that it is possible for *anyone* to have year-round pleasure from plants, then I shall feel richly rewarded.

I am particularly grateful to Helen Wilson who convinced me that my experiences might encourage more people to enjoy this rewarding hobby, and for her inspiration and encouragement to the completion of my task; to Mr. and Mrs. Burnham Bowden, William Meacham, Andrew J. Raskopf, and Howard Cross for advice and special assistance; to Lord & Burnham, Division of Burnham Corporation, for information on greenhouse structures, heating systems, and all of the color and black-and-white photographs in this book except those otherwise credited; and to *Under Glass*, the home greenhouse gardener's magazine, for access to and use of pertinent articles and information.

My gratitude, also, to Helen Krieg for a tremendous amount of perfect typing; to my artist, John R. Snyder, for his line drawings of my actual greenhouse methods and equipment; to Jack Kramer for his careful checking of my discussion of orchids; and to my nieces, Mary Louise and Margaret, who cheerfully gave up many a bedtime story hour for "Aunt Claire's book."

White Plains, New York   CLAIRE L. BLAKE
January, 1967

Part One

Get Set!

2. Even a "quick-bite" breakfast becomes an enjoyable meal in this delightful setting. (ROCHE PHOTO)

1

Joys of a Garden Under Glass

For all who love plants and flowers, nothing is more intriguing, more stimulating, than growing them in a garden under glass. When the north wind whistles and the snowflakes cling, when panes go opaque as temperate climate confronts zero, your greenhouse is a place of utter delight, fun to work in, a joy to contemplate, with a wealth of beauty and fragrance to share.

There is always a certain suspenseful excitement about a greenhouse. True, you remember what you have planted, but when you open the door in the morning, you never know quite what to expect. Yesterday when you left it, your greenhouse may have been full of bright promise. Overnight, a miracle has occurred and morning reveals a fairyland of color—delicate pink points on swelling camellia buds, ruffled cerise ballerinas on the tips of the cactus; unfolding white, yellow, and lavender orchids, an African-violet shaping up well for the show, and white hyacinths pouring fragrance into the aisle.

Greenhouse gardening offers excitement at any time, but nothing equals the thrill of your *first* "winter garden." Even the most familiar plants take on new beauty under glass. A favorite geranium is no longer just a geranium, but a brilliant splash of crimson on a gray winter day—a lift to the spirits of a shut-in, a brighter table for your holiday entertaining.

If this is your first experience with growing plants, you will know a certain kind of wonder: seeds like specks of dust grow into spikes of

3. Gardening under glass is especially pleasant at night.

lemon-yellow, pink, and white snapdragons; shriveled beads produce nasturtiums in myriad colors, gold through mahogany. From tangled straw-colored aerial roots come 3- to 4-foot stems supporting miniature orchids in vivid orange, and these will open continuously for many months. From lumpy tubers will emerge velvet-textured gloxinias; the stiff and shiny flowers of anthuriums will look more lacquered than real. Each new type of growth seems more amazing than what went before; each effort more rewarding. After years of under-glass gardening, the first December blossoms are still exciting; in a greenhouse you never become insensitive to beauty, you are never a seasoned veteran. Indeed, there is no end to the possibilities of enjoyment—and no surer way to good health. Go into your greenhouse with a headache, and you come out humming a tune. Take in a problem and it will be solved as you work with your plants.

Men are likely to be attracted to hybridizing, air-layering, and grafting or they may want to specialize on some hobby plant—orchids, begonias, or camellias. Women, usually, are more interested in flowers to cut for the house or for arrangements to enter at flower shows; or perhaps in growing something exotic not readily found at the florist's shop. Children are fascinated by what happens to the seeds they sow. In a greenhouse there is excitement and satisfaction for everybody. Each time seeds are sown, bulbs planted, cuttings made, or leaves set down to root, you have a feeling of anticipation. When the first green tip breaks through the soil, or bulb spears get green, it is unbelievably fascinating. As you watch true leaves form on seedlings, as each small plant develops, you sense an affinity for this child of nature that is your own to care for right up to the rewarding fullness of colorful maturity.

4. Flowers in the greenhouse in the dead of winter!

If you have gardened out-of-doors, you know something of this wonder and pleasure, but in your garden under glass you will find that plants are even more fun, for in a greenhouse you are close to every process of growth, and the contrast with the outside world in its long winter pause is striking indeed. And there is another advantage. In some seasons, outdoor gardens prove more frustrating than delightful. After you have cultivated, fertilized, watered, and sprayed, months of debilitating drought may occur, or a single rain storm may wreak havoc with your choicest blooms.

Under glass, it is a different story: you are in complete control of environment. You are always sure of your reward no matter what the weather, and in a greenhouse your flowers can complete their normal life span, while you enjoy them to the fullest.

5. This 3-bench greenhouse produces more than enough seedlings and cuttings for the surrounding garden.

6. Greenhouse used as a pleasing entrance to home or garden. (GOTTSCHO-SCHLEISNER PHOTO)

If you are a beginner, gardening under glass will excite you; if you are an experienced gardener, the greater possibilities will be a delight. Either way, there is something about greenhouse gardening that gets to you. Once you understand the fundamentals, you discover how little the effort, how big the results, and you become a devotee like the rest of us who are satisfied with no less than flowers for twelve months of the year.

> *Who loves a garden loves a greenhouse too.*
> *Unconscious of a less propitious clime,*
> *There blooms exotic beauty, warm and snug,*
> *While the winds whistle, and the snows descend.*
> WILLIAM COWPER

2

The Choice Is Yours—
Types and Styles of Greenhouses

Now that you have decided to have a greenhouse, you will want to investigate the numerous types and styles offered by various firms—some long established, others comparatively new—offering the latest in greenhouse construction. If you have nurtured your desire for a garden under glass for some time, you will probably have definite ideas as to just where and how you would like to build it. You will do well, however, to make haste slowly and not to let yourself be carried away simply because you have finally made the momentous decision.

First send for the catalogues of two or three firms whose advertisements you will find in garden magazines. Study these catalogues, noting particularly the construction features stressed by each manufacturer. You will find that some features are exclusive with certain firms, that some seem to be offered by all of them. Yet there will be small differences in construction that can make one greenhouse superior to others for *your* particular use.

You may be surprised by the number of types, styles, and sizes of greenhouses available. Perhaps you will be perplexed by the jargon of the trade: *ridge* refers to the central and highest member of the roof of the glass structure; the *eave* is the definite break your eye encounters as it travels from ridge to ground. In standard construction, an unbroken line goes from eave to *sill*. The sill rests upon a *wall* that may be made of masonry (poured concrete, cement blocks, cinder blocks, bricks, or decorative rocks or stones set in concrete); of wood reinforced with steel; or of wood reinforced with wood. All kinds of walls, including the glass sides of a glass-to-ground design, rest on *footings,* which may be of poured concrete, steel, or redwood or cypress. Footings extend from *grade* (ground level), or a couple of inches above grade, down to *frost level* or a few inches below frost level. Your local building department will tell you the official frost level for your area; if your building codes require that you have a permit to erect a greenhouse, your footings *must* go down to the official frost level, and they should anyway so that alternating freezing and thawing of the ground will not heave your greenhouse up and out of alignment.

7. Sectional construction in numerous styles and sizes adapts to any location.

8. The graceful curved eaves of this sectionalized hobby greenhouse are enhanced by attractive planters.

Which greenhouse for you?

The type of greenhouse you select depends upon the amount of money you want to spend, the location and space available, whether you are likely to be permanently content with a small house or will want to expand later; whether you plan to use your greenhouse exclusively for growing plants or expect to furnish part of it as a living or family room; the plants you want to grow now and in the future, reconciliation with the surroundings (trees and the architecture of your home), sunlight, and details of construction and installation.

There are two basic greenhouse categories: *free-standing* and *attached.* A free-standing greenhouse is always *even-span,* while an attached greenhouse may be *even-span* or *lean-to.*

9. Camellia hobbyists or rose growers find glass-to-ground models ideal. Pots, tubs, or ground beds allow plenty of headroom for tall shrubs.

Free-standing greenhouse: An independent, detached, self-supported glass structure that has two sides and two ends; it must have a door in one end and may have a door in each end. The heat, water, and light that must be provided may involve expensive installation costs if these facilities must be extended some distance from your residence.

Attached greenhouse: A glass structure that is connected to your residence, garage, or other solid building on your property; it may be an even-span greenhouse with one end connected to a building, or it may be a lean-to greenhouse. A greenhouse attached to your home is easier to tend and less costly to heat; the care and pleasure of plants are more readily shared, and you can enjoy your tasks even in inclement weather without having to go out into the cold. An attached greenhouse is made easily accessible through removal of a portion of a house wall or the installation of a door. Warmth from the living area can supplement that provided for the greenhouse, thus reducing heating costs. In an attached greenhouse, electric and water lines are easily connected to the house supply

Even-span type: A balanced structure, alike on both sides from eave to sill, the glass covering an area large enough for at least two growing benches with a center walk between. An even-span greenhouse has the advantage of providing about twice as much growing area as a lean-to at only a moderate additional cost. When it is attached to your home, the greater part of the structure extends out from the house and adequate summer ventilation is more easily provided than in an attached lean-to. Or, the even-span greenhouse may be a free-standing structure.

Lean-to type: Half of an even-span greenhouse—and, as the name implies, this type is attached (along the ridge line) to another structure, usually your residence, for support. The lean-to may be built along the side of a main building or fitted into the angle of an ell, or it can be butted against porch or patio. Essential for flowering plants

10. The growing area in this lean-to greenhouse is doubled because the glass walls allow planting under benches.

is a location that provides a minimum of three hours of winter sunshine. Lean-to greenhouses cost less than the even-span type because
there are fewer structural members and the supporting wall is already
provided. They are ideal when space is limited.

Perhaps no one greenhouse can be the best. There are advantages to
both types of construction. The even-span has double the growing area
of a lean-to, but the lean-to is less expensive.

Which style?

Once you have decided on the type of greenhouse that is best for
you, you can consider the various styles. The glass sides of most hobby
greenhouses slope outward gently from eave to sill, and this avoids the
look of a commercial greenhouse. A slope-sided greenhouse, with its
lower roof pitch and low silhouette, blends well with residential architecture or is an attractive highlight for the garden. And sloping sides

11. Simply designed for do-it-yourself assembly, this little lean-to greenhouse is practical for the gardener whose time is limited.

12. The even-span counterpart of the lean-to in Figure 11 is 9 feet wide. Green vinyl shading is attractive.

give you a cultural advantage over straight sides: they transmit more light from the winter sun when it is low on the horizon.

There are also two types of eaves, straight or curved. For growing, one type is as good as the other, but your home may be more enhanced by straight eaves than by the curved type, and this will help you to decide. However, curved eaves have a softer look that may blend with your architecture instead of appearing to be a stark addition to it. The choice here is really your personal preference.

Construction

As a rule, hobby greenhouses are prefabricated, usually in maintenance-free aluminum, though some West Coast firms make models of redwood. Both kinds are structurally designed for the do-it-yourself

13. This 10-foot wide prefabricated aluminum hobby greenhouse is attractive when built as a free-standing structure in a garden area.

gardener and, of course, they cost less than custom-built models. Folks handy with tools can assemble one of these prefabricated greenhouses in a few weekends, or a local contractor can erect it for you at a reasonable cost. Greenhouses are delivered ready for installation, but most manufacturers recommend that masonry, plumbing, and electrical work be done by professionals.

An ideal hobby greenhouse includes wide sections of glass for maximum transmission of sunlight, a system of condensation control to prevent unsightly accumulation of moisture on structural members (and an eventual unhealthy dripping onto plants and fixtures), and regulated roof ventilation to provide the very best growing conditions. Glazing may use standard putty or modern vinyl plastics (called dry glazing), depending on the manufacturer. Keep in mind that heat loss through inadequate glazing can be costly.

Location

Manufacturers recommend south, southeast, or southwest exposures for attached even-span or lean-to greenhouses, a south exposure being the best. A west exposure is acceptable if no other location is available,

14. The model in Figure 13 is equally handsome and workable when it is attached to your home.

but summer shade is essential to protect delicate plants from the burning rays of the afternoon sun.

If the only spot you have for your greenhouse faces north, do not give up the idea of a winter garden. Foliage plants grow well without direct sun, and shade-loving plants such as African-violets and orchids also thrive in such an exposure *provided it is fully light.* (A north-facing greenhouse could include fluorescent lights for sun-loving plants.) However, heating costs are higher in a greenhouse with a north exposure.

15. This 7-foot wide prefabricated aluminum lean-to greenhouse (above) fits nicely under a low house eave and takes up very little garden area.

16. The curved-eave lean-to (right) is 9 feet 8 inches wide, with room for two benches.

Glass-to-ground greenhouses

The need for extra growing space within the available basic greenhouse sizes has resulted in the glass-to-ground design that is offered by several manufacturers. In this design, solid walls from sill to ground are replaced by glass, practically doubling the growing area. Camellia hobbyists admire this glass-to-ground design because it insures adequate light for their tall plants, and it is practical to remove the standard benches.

17. This 4-section lean-to greenhouse complements the architectural style of the residence and is a pleasing addition to the patio area.

Fiberglass-reinforced plastic

Increasing in popularity is the use of fiberglass-reinforced plastic instead of glass for greenhouse roof and walls. The translucent corrugated type is preferred. The color will depend on the plants you grow, because different colors transmit different amounts of light and also different parts of the light spectrum. The most translucent white fiberglass-reinforced plastic you can get is probably the best for a hobby greenhouse. Extensive research is being carried on by agricultural experiment stations and greenhouse manufacturers to determine how successful such structures will be for hobby and commercial growers.

A family room

Besides being a place to grow plants, part of your greenhouse can be furnished to serve as a family room. Any type or style of greenhouse can be adapted provided there is adequate control of condensation. A lean-to that adjoins an open porch or basement playroom can be arranged attractively as a garden room with slate floors, built-in

18. Excavating to provide headroom solves the problem of low-eave, low-wall construction of a lean-to greenhouse.

pool, or cabinets topped with planting trays instead of conventional greenhouse benches. Even-span models can be more completely furnished as sitting or dining areas with waterproof carpeting, easy chairs, game or dining tables, and draperies or bamboo shades to avoid the "living-in-a-glass-house" feeling.

19. Sectional construction allows an even-span greenhouse to be fitted around the corner of a house, and the addition of a fill-in section to accommodate door into residence.

20. Slanted sides with glass to the ground provide maximum light for growing plants in this lean-to greenhouse. Construction is inexpensive as a masonry wall is not required.

Grow into your greenhouse—not out of it!

Before you buy a greenhouse, you should decide upon the best location, the type and style suited to your architecture and your kind of gardening, and the greenhouse size. One thing is certain—and on this all hobby greenhouse enthusiasts are agreed—you had better put up a bigger house than you now think you will need. Do not select a very small greenhouse just because you are a beginner. Seeds germinate fast, enthusiasm grows faster still, and the small greenhouse that seemed ample in the planning stage too soon becomes cramped and crowded. So give yourself room to grow in, and then grow *into* your greenhouse, not out of it!

21. The slanted sides in this glass-to-ground even-span free-standing green-house give extra growing space in the under-bench area.

3

Climate Control

Next to be considered are the technical aspects of greenhouse operation: temperature, heat, ventilation, water, shade, light.

THREE RANGES OF TEMPERATURE

When cultural directions for plants include growing temperatures, these refer to night temperatures, unless there is specific advice for germination of seeds or rooting of cuttings under special conditions. It is usual to run a greenhouse in one of three general ranges:

Cool greenhouse	45–50 F
Moderate greenhouse	55–60 F
Warm greenhouse	65–70 F

Of course, it is not possible to maintain the entire greenhouse at exactly the specified range, and this is an advantage. For within each range, it is possible to provide widely different climatic conditions. When you run a check with several strategically placed thermometers, you will find that there are pockets, sections, corners, and high and low locations where the temperature varies five to ten degrees from the general setting. In these areas you can indulge yourself with a plant or two from the list recommended for the moderate greenhouse even though you run your house cool; or you can have success with plants on the moderate list although most of your plants are grown warm.

You will discover that corners are warmer than the center of the greenhouse, and that rising heat results in more warmth at head height above benches—a good place for hanging baskets or shelves for orchids. If yours is a glass-to-ground greenhouse, you will surely have some cool, humid areas even in a moderate-to-warm greenhouse, as moisture from above and below the benches combines with the rising heat. Furthermore, recommended temperatures for various plants often "straddle" two ranges, and many plants can be grown in a cool *or* moderate house, or in a moderate *or* warm house. Obviously, then, you have considerable leeway in your selection of compatible plants for any one of the three rather arbitrary temperature ranges.

In my own greenhouse with a night temperature setting of 52 F, in February I usually have in bloom camellias, cattleya and cymbidium orchids, Christmas cactus, crown-of-thorns, geraniums, and fibrous-rooted begonias. Coming along nicely will be amaryllis, gloxinias, tuberous begonias and maybe a dendrobium orchid or two in bud.

Each temperature range has its advantages but this cool greenhouse —45–50 F at night—is the one I prefer, and of course it costs the least for heating. The low night temperature does not preclude a pleasant warm daytime atmosphere when the sun makes the house a most agreeable place to work. And the cool house marvelously prolongs the life of flowers. The same cyclamen in bud and flower before Christmas will continue in handsome bloom through April.

The temperature range best suited to the plants you want to grow will directly affect your decision about the heating equipment you will buy for your greenhouse. (Lists of plants for each temperature range are given in Part IV.)

HEAT

How to heat your greenhouse is the big decision, not so much in terms of installation and operation but in the selection of the kind of heat most economical for your type of greenhouse and its particular location. Efficiency and economy are possible with any fuel—gas, oil, or electricity—if properly selected and utilized, and with either system —warm-air or hot-water. At one time, only hot water was considered a practical means of providing adequate, evenly distributed heat. Pipes were run under the benches and around the entire greenhouse. But research proved that warm-air systems, as they have been developed for today's greenhouses, are just as effective for small greenhouses.

No matter what the system or the fuel, several factors determine the amount of heat required. These are the size and location of your greenhouse, whether it is attached or detached, the minimum night temperature necessary for the plants you want to grow, and the severity of the winter in your area. Also, costs may vary somewhat from season to season, depending on the weather in a particular year.

No matter *where* you live, if you plan year-round operation, some means of heating is necessary, even though most or all of the heat required during the day is furnished by the sun. In southern states, small gas units or electric heaters are adequate for even a fairly large hobby greenhouse, since outside temperatures are not usually so low as in the North. Even in the Deep South, where both days and nights are warm, auxiliary heat should be provided to offset the occasional drop in temperature that brings a few chilling and possibly freezing nights.

Selecting a heater

Before selecting a heater, check the electric and gas rates in your locality. It may be more economical to use electricity because of low kilowatt-hour rates, or gas may cost less than you suppose. However, don't try to economize on the heater itself—only the *best* is good enough in the long run. Greenhouse manufacturers or local contractors will tell you the ratings of various heaters. They can also estimate the amount of heat in BTU's necessary to adequately maintain the night temperature you want in a greenhouse of given size. Some greenhouse catalogues include tables for calculating the BTU's (British Thermal Units) required per hour. These are calculated on the basis of an outside night temperature of zero F and a specified inside night temperature, with conversion factors given to enable you to figure correctly for your own conditions, in case your outside temperature does not drop to zero F or you desire an inside night temperature other than that specified in the BTU tables.

Select a heater that will furnish slightly more BTU's than you figure will be required. Extra cost at the time of purchase will be nominal, but you may need the safety margin if your greenhouse is in an extremely windy location. Also, if later you decide to increase the size of your greenhouse, or to grow plants that need a higher night temperature, you will probably not have to change your heater.

What will be the cost of heat to maintain a certain constant temperature throughout the growing year? Quite a bit less than most gardeners imagine. In most sections of the country heat must be furnished during the cold months, starting in October and tapering off in April. Through late fall and early spring when days are quite sunny, you will usually have to furnish heat only from sunset to sunrise, as the sun will provide the heat required through the day. This makes for a considerable saving in heating costs. My second greenhouse, 13 by 15 feet, maintained a 55 F night temperature some eight months for an average of $100 for the entire season—much less than I had anticipated in the Westchester suburbs, north of New York City.

At this point, a special caution is appropriate. If you live where power failures occur frequently, you might like to investigate a heater with a built-in *non-electric* thermostat. If you prefer a heater without this safety device, then an automatic warning system and some kind of auxiliary heating equipment for use during an emergency will serve you well.

In a greenhouse with automatic ventilation, a gas heater—if it requires installation of a chimney—must also be automatically controlled by a thermostat. When roof vents open, warm air flows up and out of the greenhouse, causing a down-draft of outside air through the chimney. If the heater is operating at the time of the down-draft, noxious fumes and other combustion products are spread through the greenhouse, possibly resulting in damage to plants and danger to anyone working there. If the heater and the ventilators are operated automatically—each controlled by its own thermostat at different settings —the heater cannot function when the ventilators are open. Thus the hazard is eliminated.

Electric heaters

Easy to install, completely automatic, an electric heater is ideal for the small hobby greenhouse or for a cool compartment in a larger partitioned greenhouse. The electric heater is placed under the bench at one end of the greenhouse but angled to blow heat the entire length of the structure. The heater should have a built-in circulation fan to distribute warm air evenly throughout the greenhouse. A thermostat with a range of 40 to 80 F and a separate heavy-duty electric line are necessary; heater and thermostats should be installed at the time of greenhouse erection in accordance with local electric codes.

Warm-air gas-fired heaters

Two types of warm-air gas-fired heaters have proved satisfactory for the hobby greenhouse; one requires a chimney, the other does not.

A compact unit space-heater, AGA (American Gas Association) approved, is adequate for a small to medium-sized greenhouse, say up to 10 to 18 feet long. It comes equipped with a safety pilot and, ideally, with electric or non-electric thermostatic control. A metal smokepipe or masonry chimney will have to be provided. Install the heater at the end of the greenhouse walk against the gable and away from the door, so the chimney or smokepipe can be carried up and out without reducing your growing area. Larger heaters can be equipped with an electric blower-fan kit to assure circulation of warm air through the greenhouse.

The other, a non-vented heater, requires no chimney; the combustion chamber is sealed off *outside* the greenhouse. Only outside air is used; no noxious fumes are combusted into the greenhouse and plants and gardeners are entirely safe. The heater is usually installed in the wall-gable end or side, and extends only 8½ inches into the greenhouse. The largest size needs only a 17- by 20-inch wall opening. My second greenhouse was heated satisfactorily with such a heater, but we positioned it on the sill in place of one light of glass in the center gable panel and closed the opening with a filler panel of aluminum. A special fan-control switch prevents circulation of cold outside air before the heater has warmed it sufficiently to assure draft-free distribution of heat. The heater is AGA approved and comes with a safety pilot and high-limit gas shut-off switch. Cabinet is of welded construction with a heat-exchanger guaranteed against burnout for five years.

Warm-air oil-fired heaters

A warm-air oil-fired heater with a 100,000 BTU output is available. This is large enough to heat a 25-foot-long greenhouse. The heater is 23 inches high, 72 inches long, and 22 inches deep, and is designed to fit underneath a greenhouse bench. The gun-type oil burner comes equipped with all controls, and a special thermostat with sunshade. The built-in blower has a rating of 900 cubic feet per minute, to assure good air circulation. A masonry chimney 12 to 24 inches above the ridge, or a metal smokepipe with rotary cap to help provide adequate draft, should be provided. Standard household fuel oil can be used. If the heater is installed in an attached workroom, a return air duct is required.

Utilizing your residential heating system

For an attached greenhouse, or for a detached unit no farther than 50 feet from your residence boiler, you may find it practical to adapt your present heating system to include the greenhouse. One greenhouse manufacturer offers a Heating Extension Kit for this purpose. It can be used on a hot-water or steam installation to provide an independent, thermostatically controlled second zone of heat for the greenhouse. With this extension, it is not necessary to replace your present boiler or to add a second unit for the greenhouse. Installation costs are moderate. This extension provides one of the least expensive greenhouse heating systems, and it does not reduce the heat available for your home. With it you will be operating a two-zone system, each with its own thermostatic control.

If you are considering this extension of an existing heating system, have your local heating contractor check the BTU output of your present boiler to be sure there is sufficient capacity for the extra demand.

With a low-pressure steam-boiler, the boiler is tapped below the water line to provide the greenhouse heat. Install an aquastat on the boiler to maintain a minimum of 180 F water temperature inside; also install a high-duty circulator. This system provides hot-water heat for the greenhouse and steam heat for your home. The hot water is circulated throughout the greenhouse by means of fin-tube radiation. With hot-water systems the aquastat is set high enough to maintain water in the boiler at 180 F or higher. Most forced-circulation systems will do this. Low-temperature gravity-flow hot-water systems are not suitable for use with extension kits, and a vacuum-steam system cannot be adapted to two-zone heating. When you extend a heating system to a detached unit, all heating lines between house and greenhouse are buried in a trench to a depth below the local frost level.

If your home has a warm-air system that you wish to utilize for the greenhouse, it will be wise to attach your greenhouse to your house and as close to the furnace as possible. Supply and return ducts for warm and cold air must cover the shortest possible distance between furnace and greenhouse. Motor-operated damper controls are necessary in the heating ducts of both home and greenhouse. Each should be controlled by its own thermostat so as to operate independently. If you find the warm-air supply is too drying for the greenhouse, install some sort of humidifier, or compensate for the drying out by extra watering and syringing of plants.

Heating extension kits can be used for glass-to-ground designs or in partitioned greenhouses but extra pipe or finned tube for additional radiation is necessary.

Most greenhouse manufacturers and local heating contractors have BTU tables, conversion factors, and other information for estimating sizes and ratings of boilers, heating systems, and heaters for greenhouse use. Don't decide on a heater or the conversion of a system without consulting one of these specialists. An error in judgment can be costly.

Alarms and auxiliary heat

Every greenhouse heating system should be operated with an alarm system to sound a warning if the temperature falls below or rises above a pre-determined setting. A lean-to attached to a friend's home seemed safe "for the time being" and installation of a warning system was delayed. One night the temperature unexpectedly dropped to below freezing, and she lost her entire orchid collection in a matter of hours. I was more fortunate! The one time my heater failed, it apparently went out about an hour before my usual morning visit. When I checked, the thermometer registered 32 F, but at that time my greenhouse was filled mostly with cymbidium orchids that can endure such cold *temporarily*. I did lose one cattleya orchid, and certainly would have lost more if the failure had occurred during the night and the plants had been chilled for a longer time. Installation of an alarm system is simple. A high-low temperature alarm, battery-operated, can be set to sound a warning bell or buzzer in your home whenever the temperature reaches a danger point.

It is always a good idea to have available some means of auxiliary heat. A small kerosene heater will do, and it is simple to use as a temporary measure. Thermostats available for kerosene heaters are not calibrated properly for greenhouse use, so remember that if you have automatic ventilation you will have to operate it by hand during the time you are using a manually controlled kerosene heater. In an emergency when no means of auxiliary heat is available, cover plants with newspaper or plastic. If the heat failure is of brief duration, this may work. Obviously, such covering will not save plants if the greenhouse is without heat for an extended period.

In any case, schedule a summer check-up of your heating system every year. Minor adjustments made at this time—when the heat is turned off—prevent serious winter trouble. Don't let efficient operation give you a false sense of security. My own difficulty occurred because I neglected the check-up. My heater had operated reliably for five years. The one failure was due to a deposit of carbon that eventually extinguished the pilot light. A summer check-up would have revealed this and avoided a dangerous situation. Don't take your heater for granted. Check it before it checks out!

VENTILATION

Gardening under glass requires provision for circulation of air and control of temperature during hot weather as well as when the heat is on. Methods of ventilation range from a simple built-in wall sash to an automatic, thermostatically controlled roof system. When excessive heat from the sun or an artificial source is trapped inside the glass structure, the heat rises and the air stratifies—it is warm near the roof, cooler down through the house toward the floor. Then air becomes stagnant, moisture is not evaporated properly, and it is difficult to maintain a constant temperature. For this reason, some means of ventilation and air circulation must be provided.

Since hot air is trapped under the ridge, the logical place for an opening to relieve the concentration is along the ridge, ideally along the full length of the structure. These openings, or roof sash, can be regulated by push rods, by manual gears, or automatically by thermostatic control.

Push-rod-operated roof sash

In the sectionalized hobby greenhouses, most push-rod-operated roof sash cover two sections alternately—two operative, two stationary. Some models provide push-rod sash in side panels only, with only one panel operative. (The rods are the type used on basement sash in the home—a flat metal rod fastened to the window allows it to be pushed open and held in place when a hole in the rod is slipped over a fixed pin on the bottom rail of the sash opening.) Several holes are provided in the rod. The amount of ventilation depends upon the distance the rod is pushed out before a hole is fitted over the pin.

Manually operated roof sash

The next-best method of ventilation is by manually operated gears. Here again, sash is placed along the ridge line of the greenhouse, each sash fastened to a pipe shaft that is centered through a rotary gear with a continuous leather strap or chain. Pulling on the strap or chain activates the gear that operates the sash, opening or closing it to the degree desired. The number of turns regulates the amount of ventilation. Each gear operator controls one line of ridge sash; long runs of sash are divided into two or more shorter units.

The drawbacks to either push-rod or manual types of ventilation lie in the temperature variation inside the greenhouse, which in turn depends upon the weather outside, the amount of sun, and the intensity and direction of the wind. As these affect the inside temperature, frequent changes of sash opening are necessary. Constant attention to these fluctuations is a chore if an even temperature is to be maintained, and if the greenhouse must be left unattended for some time, plants may be damaged seriously.

Automatic ventilation

Most hobby greenhouses now come with automatic controls. A moisture-proof thermostat, set 10 degrees higher than the setting of the night-temperature thermostat, regulates the sash electrically. There is now available a motor that provides automatic ventilation for pennies a day; it uses only 10 watts per motor when sash are open and it has a built-in safety device that closes the roof sash if electric power fails, thus retaining heat in the greenhouse until current is restored. Each motor will lift about 5 feet of sash; therefore multiple motors will be required, depending on the length of the greenhouse.

The thermostat that regulates the vent sash is placed above the bench line at about the center of the area in which a given temperature is to be maintained. It can be suspended on electric conduit from a roof bar, or it can be installed on a pipe stand permanently attached to a bench. In either place, the thermostat must be protected from direct sunlight or blasts from the heater. An aluminum shade around back, sides, and over the top of the thermostat is the most practical protection, but there must be an air-circulation space between the shade and the thermostat. The same *type* of thermostat can be used to control both heat and ventilation, but there must be a *separate* one for each operation.

Automatic systems open and close the sash as often as is necessary to maintain the temperature setting.

Where summers are very hot and the greenhouse is used all year, additional ventilation is helpful. Built-in wall sash, push-rod operated, will give under-bench air circulation without direct drafts on plants; this type of sash can also be installed at the eave line. If you want to provide extra air circulation and dress up your greenhouse at the same time, replace one or more glass sections in the side or gable end with hand-operated jalousies (overlapping horizontal glass slats set in an aluminum frame).

Complete climate-control system

The ultimate in greenhouse ventilation is now available with climate-control systems. Regardless of the weather, you need not lift a finger to control ventilation, humidity, or summer cooling. One system utilizes a 12-inch exhaust fan mounted in one end or in one side of the greenhouse in a clear plastic panel. The fan is equipped with a built-in shutter and safety backguard, and is automatically controlled by a thermostat. When temperature rises above the setting, the fan operates thermostatically to force out hot air. Cool air is pulled in and through the greenhouse by means of a large jalousie installed in the opposite end or side. This system provides one complete change of air per minute.

For semi-automatic operation, the volume of incoming air can be hand controlled: the jalousie is fully opened in summer, only partly opened in cool weather. For complete automatic ventilation, you simply install a thermostatically activated motor to open the jalousie. When the proper temperature is achieved, the motor will shut off the fan and close the jalousie.

A more complete climate-control system utilizes two thermostatically controlled jalousies at one end of the greenhouse, one jalousie above the other. They open and close automatically as temperature fluctuates. Cool air, drawn through the lower jalousie by a two-speed 16-inch fan, circulates through the greenhouse and is forced out through the upper jalousie. An aluminum air-control cabinet is placed in front of the lower jalousie to serve as a mixing chamber, warming the cool outside air by mixing it with warm greenhouse air before it is circulated, to prevent sudden temperature changes harmful to plants.

For maximum summer ventilation, you set the fan at high speed and adjust the control damper in the cabinet to bring in enough outside air to provide up to one-and-a-half complete air changes per minute. For winter operation, you close the lower jalousie and set the fan at slow speed to recirculate the warm greenhouse air without introducing cold outside air.

To air condition your greenhouse in summer, and to provide year-round humidity control, a built-in mist spray attachment is included. An electric valve regulated by a humidistat controls the flow of water to a mist-fog nozzle mounted on the front of the fan cabinet. When the greenhouse air gets too dry, the fog nozzle produces a fine mist that is circulated throughout the greenhouse by the air fan. Thus humidity can be automatically regulated and maintained throughout the year.

My first greenhouse was thus climate-controlled and my snapdragons were the finest I have ever grown. My second greenhouse did not have a complete-control system, but it did have automatic ventilation. Night temperature was maintained at 55 F, and after some experimenting with manual operation of the vents in very cold weather, I found that setting the vent thermostat 20 degrees higher than the heat thermostat (instead of the usual 10 degree differential) kept the greenhouse adequately supplied with fresh air without harm to plants. Unless the day was extremely warm and sunny, the thermostat did not open vents often enough to cause excessive changes in temperature. Since I had to leave my greenhouse unattended during the day, this proved a satisfactory arrangement. In warm weather, the differential between heat and vent thermostat settings was returned to 10 degrees, since more circulation was required and the warmer outside air was no cause for concern.

My present greenhouse has modified climate control. It is equipped with air-control cabinet, fan, and jalousies, but no mist nozzle. Instead, a galvanized tray 20 by 24 by 1½ inches deep, placed in front of the air-control cabinet, is kept filled with water. This evaporates and is circulated through the air by the fan. Considerable humidity is thus provided and it is augmented by an occasional hose spraying of walks to produce lovely cymbidium and cattleya orchids.

In extremely warm weather, additional ventilation can always be provided by replacing the solid glass panel in the door with jalousie or screen or both.

WATER

How much and how often to water plants always puzzles the beginner, and there is no definite rule to follow. No one amount of water can be said to be right for pot plants, bench plants, or seedlings. Types of potting and benching soils; the amount of sunshine, humidity, and air circulation; the season of the year; and the location of the greenhouse are all factors in developing a watering program conducive to steady, healthy growth and bloom. Experience has produced some helpful fundamental practices, but don't be so influenced by these that you are afraid to depart from a schedule—this would be a mistake. Theoretically, water should be applied in the morning, preferably not later than noon, and on a rising temperature, because when you water plants there is a sudden drop in temperature. This causes moisture in the air to condense, forming droplets of water on foliage and flowers. If there is not enough time before darkness for this moisture to evaporate, conditions conducive to disease are created. But this is a *general* rule, so be guided accordingly.

On occasion, if you find your seedlings drying out, or your primroses and hydrangeas wilting in the afternoon, have no qualms about watering them at once. You may also find that some plants always need extra water, and at odd times, to keep them healthy. If you go to business during the day, you may sometimes have to skip morning watering. On checking your greenhouse in the evening, if you find plants looking fairly dry and you doubt that they should be left until the next morning for watering, by all means water them, even if it is night time. But be careful not to splash foliage, and don't be heavy-handed; this is only a tide-over watering to be completed the next morning.

Plants absorb water from soil by means of their roots; some of the water is used in food manufacture, the rest is transpired (given back to the air) through the foliage. Too much water is to be avoided, particularly for seedlings and new cuttings, for these have very fine root hairs that quickly die if they are compressed by wet soil from which all oxygen has been eliminated. That is why sharp sand, vermiculite, or sphagnum moss are recommended for seeds and cuttings. The nature of these mediums prevents water pressure from packing themselves around tiny new roots. Misting or light spraying of cuttings is also beneficial. The mist replaces moisture transpired through the leaves, cools plants by evaporation, and helps roots become established before they must take on the job of completely supplying plants with both water and food.

Keep in mind that soils differ in consistency. A loose, sandy soil holds moisture only a short time. Soils that are heavy or clayey pack and hold water longer, even to the point of sogginess. Obviously, plants in sandy soil require more water to become fully moist while those in heavy soil require less water. Plants in clay pots require more water than those in plastic containers because clay pots themselves absorb water. Plastic is not water absorbent and it keeps air from reaching the soil to dry it out.

On sunny days or during the period when the heat is turned on, repeated waterings may be necessary because heat makes soil dry out quite rapidly. During cool rainy spells, soil dries out slowly and less water is needed. As you see, only suggestions, not rules, can be given to help with your watering schedule; much depends upon circumstances. Like the rest of us, you will have to rely upon a certain amount of trial and error to establish a satisfactory procedure. In any case, it is better to err on the side of too little than too much. If a plant dries out slightly between waterings, even to the point of wilting, it is easier to perk it up and keep it healthy than to revive it if heavy hosing has packed soil around roots and cut off their supply of oxygen, which often proves fatal to the plant.

Be patient; use common sense. You will be surprised how quickly you will "get the feel" of the soil and overcome your qualms about watering too much or too little. And once you do get the feel of it, you will find it takes less time to take care of all your plants.

Master-control watering systems

If you install a master-control system of watering, the whole business is simplified. For bench plants, a length of plastic hose—perforated the entire length with minute openings—can be attached to a faucet and laid on the soil between the plants. When water is needed, you simply turn on the faucet far enough to force water through the openings and then leave it on until soil is well soaked. A more permanent arrangement consists of fastening a flexible plastic pipe with spray nozzles around the perimeter of the bench area. Either method can be controlled automatically by an electric water valve and a 24-hour time clock. The clock, wired in series with the valve for automatic operation, is set to control the duration of the watering cycle.

A new system for watering pot plants as well as bench plants is now available in kit form. A molded rubber distributor is placed between the pots, and water is supplied directly to each pot through hollow plastic tubes attached to the distributor. Tubes are approximately 5 feet long, and are easily held in place in the pot by a lead weight at the end. Small plants or pots take one tube; two or more are necessary for large pots, seed flats, or big benched plants. A kit contains two water distributors with 20 outlet tubes each, and one 10-foot length of hose to connect the distributors.

This system may be made automatic with time-clock control, and one manufacturer markets a control panel for just this purpose. It includes two time clocks, an electric water valve with strainer, two hose bibbs, and an electric switch for manual or automatic operation. The panel is preassembled and ready to be plugged into a polarized 110 volt 60 cycle electric outlet. Just connect to your water supply with pipe, copper tubing, or hose, and you are ready to operate the system. With this control panel, plants can be watered individually and automatically every day. One time clock, a 24-hour type, turns the system on and off at pre-selected times, usually mid-morning. Since this 24-hour clock has a minimum operating time of 18 minutes —far too long for a watering cycle—a second fast-cycle clock is required to reduce and control the watering interval. As a rule, only a few minutes watering per day is required with a kit system. However, the duration of the watering period can be adjusted by changing the settings to suit local water pressure, weather, and greenhouse conditions. The 24-hour clock also allows for skip-a-day control, and you can set the system to water on pre-selected days. An electric switch permits manual operation when you want it. If you set the switch to "manual," water will be supplied to the entire system, taking care of all plants until you reset the switch to "automatic." The parts in the kit are assembled on exterior-grade plywood that can be mounted anywhere in the greenhouse convenient to water and electricity. The system can be enlarged and extended simply by adding extra hose bibbs.

Mist system

If you are growing orchids or other plants that benefit from periodic fine spraying, you may want to install a mist system. With this an electric valve, equipped with a strainer, controls the flow of water to the mist nozzles. The valve comes with female pipe threads on both inlet and outlet. It controls water pressure up to 150 pounds per square inch and operates on 115 volt, 60 cycle, AC current only. As in the case of the watering system described above, two time clocks are required. One 24-hour clock turns the system on during the day, off at night. The second clock, a fast-cycle repeating time clock, controls the duration of the mist cycle, usually in multiples of six seconds —six seconds on, twelve seconds off; or twelve seconds on, eighteen seconds off. It is easily adjusted to suit individual installations. Each nozzle mists an area approximately 36 inches in circumference, and you can install as many nozzles as your greenhouse requires.

If the hose used for watering is equipped with a spray nozzle, this may suffice for misting your plants, but keep the spray fine so water will evaporate quickly. If you do not have a spray nozzle, place your thumb squarely over the end of the open hose, exert an even steady pressure, and the force of the water against your thumb will produce a fine mist that can easily be directed.

Water sources

If it is impractical to furnish a water line directly to the greenhouse, get a big container—vat, barrel, tub—that can be filled from a hose attached to an outside faucet on your house. From this you can get water throughout the winter. It takes only a moment to open the inside control valve to allow the use of the hose, and to shut it off again to prevent freezing of the water line in cold weather. I had such an arrangement in my second greenhouse. A great preserving kettle, placed at the end of the center bench directly under the NoVent heater, was filled from a hose connected to the outside house supply. The blast from the heater warmed the water so there was no chilling of plants, and from the kettle a certain amount of moisture evaporated into the atmosphere. This helped overcome the inevitable drying effects of heat supplied in winter. Of course, dipping water from a kettle takes a little time, but it is a practical and economical method. Naturally you won't want to do this longer than you have to, but it is a means to an end if the greenhouse budget is tight the first year.

SHADING

In summer, greenhouses can be cooled considerably by ventilation, but the extreme heat of the sun in some sections of the country makes shading necessary. Even plants that require considerable warmth cannot stand full summer sun; they need shade or semishade for good growth and flowering. There are various means and materials for shading. Some simple installations are only temporary, others are longer lasting.

Paste or powder shading

Paste or powder shadings can be applied with sprayer, paintbrush, or roller. One gallon of paste mixed with benzine or gasoline covers about 600 square feet of glass. Two applications are necessary—one in spring when protection from sun first becomes necessary, the other toward July when the earlier application will have been almost washed away by rain. Because it weathers unevenly, paste or powder shading is always unsightly—parts of the greenhouse may be washed almost clean by spring and summer rains while protected areas of glass are still fully covered. A paint roller gives the smoothest application unless you are an expert with a sprayer. Powder shading gives briefer protection than paste, since it mixes with water and washes off more readily. Powder and paste both come in white or green. I think green is less objectionable; white looks like whitewash. (Incidentally, whitewash should never be used on an aluminum greenhouse—it contains lime that causes serious deterioration of aluminum. Either shading paste or powder may be used freely since neither contains lime.) Paste is sold by the gallon; powder comes in cartons, usually 25 pounds each. Both are cheap enough, but the cost is recurrent, since the supply has to be replenished yearly and application takes a lot of time, too.

Wood panels or aluminum slats

Wood panels or aluminum slats, made in sections to fit the glass panels of most hobby greenhouses, offer a far more attractive means of shading than paste or powder. Aluminum panel slats come in kits for easy assembling to aluminum-painted wood frames. Slotted fasteners slip over the round-head screws already in place on the greenhouse frame. Panels are easy to install in spring, quickly removed when shading is no longer necessary, and of a convenient size to store.

Panels are made for roof, sides, and the ventilator section of the greenhouse. They can be installed overall or only where they are needed, a great convenience if you are growing mixed plants with different shade requirements in the same house. Once panel shades are in place, they are usually left on all summer, and this is something of a disadvantage on sunless days when plants are deprived of much-needed light.

Wood roll-up shades

Wood roll-up shades are more practical than panels or slats. True, they are far more expensive, but they do offer the most convenient and a most attractive means of shading. Made of redwood slats linked with non-rusting metal clips, they are factory assembled and come complete with hardware, ropes, and pulleys, all ready for installation. Fastened outside just below roof ventilators, they are long enough to extend to the sill. A system of ropes and pulleys makes them easily adjustable for sun and other weather changes.

These roll-up shades usually come covered with two coats of aluminum paint to reflect the heat of the sun, but they can also be obtained unpainted if the natural redwood blends well with the color of your home, or they can be painted in some harmonizing color more attractive than a stark aluminum finish. As these shades do not cover roof ventilators, you will have to use other shading for this area if your plants require complete protection from sun. Here paste or powder will do, or a vinyl plastic; or you can hang a green netting rather like cheesecloth on the inside under the roof sash. This netting not only cuts down sunlight but if it is installed from the bottom of the roof sash on one side to the bottom of the roof sash on the other side, it also screens out insects.

Plastic shading

If you prefer plastic, try the 8 mil flexible, light-green sheet film that is proving so satisfactory. It comes in rolls 29 inches wide by 25 feet long. In my present greenhouse, two gable sections of glass were covered with it, and it still adheres nicely after twelve months even though it was left on all winter. Application is to the inside of the glass, is simple and attractive if carefully handled, and transmission of sunlight is reduced by as much as 65 per cent. The whole greenhouse may be shaded, even roof vents, and while the plastic reduces the intensity of the sun, it is sufficiently transparent for visibility into or out of the greenhouse.

To install it, cut a piece the exact size of the glass section to be covered. Then moisten the glass with a moderate stream of water from the hose or go over it with a wet sponge, making sure it is evenly moist. Place the sheet of plastic against the inside glass and smooth it down (as you would wallpaper) with a wallpaper brush, squeegee, or plastic scraper. Be sure to get rid of air bubbles and give particular attention to the corners. If the job is done properly, surface tension of water between plastic and glass holds the shading firmly in position.

When days get shorter in fall and shading is no longer needed, loosen the corners of the plastic sheets, peel them away from the glass, wipe off any moisture that remains on the plastic, and store the pieces flat. With a little care in handling, this plastic shading can be re-used for years.

Improvised shading

You may not want to buy proper shading your first summer. In that case, use your ingenuity. I have seen cheesecloth, green netting, even discarded dacron curtains, serve very well as temporary inside shading. A wire fastened along the eave line will give support to material stitched or stapled over it. Drapery rings sewn along the top edge of the material permit it to be drawn over the glass or pushed to the sides as desired.

When to apply shading

The time for application of shading varies from one section of the country to another, and is also influenced by the location of the greenhouse. Therefore, it is impossible to give definite dates; the condition of your plants will be the best indication. If soil seems to dry out unusually fast or foliage looks droopy early in the day, or seems somewhat paler than it should, it is probably time to protect plants from the gradually warming sun. Timing the removal of shading in fall is easier, for a decrease in the amount of daily sunshine is always evident, and a hint to you to get rid of any deterrent to full sun.

SUPPLEMENTAL LIGHT

Plants differ and vary in the amount of light needed to promote growth and flowering, and they have been classified according to their light requirements: plants that flower in response to longer days than nights are called *long-day* plants; those that respond to shorter days than nights are *short-day* plants; those that will flower and fruit under a wide range of day lengths are called *indeterminate* or *daylength-neutral*; those that respond to days and nights of approximately equal length are called *intermediate*.

The addition of artificial light (preferably from fluorescent lamps) to a greenhouse, is helpful in several ways. Its control can hasten or retard the development of plants at the gardener's whim; it provides light when sunlight is absent during rainy and stormy weather; it extends day length during short winter days; the space available for growing can be increased considerably by installing fluorescent lamps on the underside of waterproofed benches, thus fully utilizing the under-bench space for growing; it can turn a north-facing greenhouse that would normally accommodate only foliage plants into a flowering greenhouse.

Several excellent books on the subject of Fluorescent Light Gardening are available to help you with the mechanics of installation and to guide you in selection and use of the correct kinds of fluorescent lamps for growth of plants.

4

Growing Equipment
and Work Areas

Equipment for growing plants—as distinguished from equipment for controlling the climate—is an essential aspect of gardening under glass. You will need benches or plant trays, maybe both; pots; storage space for soil and other supplies; a convenient work area for potting; a plant-propagating area; and you will find some shelves useful. Of course, there are a few necessary tools—if you have a garden, you probably have all you will need of these. Then there is that overall classification of "sundries"—plant tags, stakes, and other useful items to make your greenhouse work easier and more fun.

Benches
What you want to grow determines the type and arrangement of benches. For plants in beds, install regulation benches at a convenient height for working, say about 2½ to 3 feet.

To make wood benches, space bottom boards of rough-sawn 1-inch-thick redwood about three-quarters of an inch apart, making the sides and ends of smooth-finished redwood. For upright and cross supports, use redwood or three-quarter-inch hot galvanized steel pipe. To insure long service in the high humidity of a greenhouse, insist on heart California redwood. Benches of standard lumber or soft wood, even when treated with a wood preservative, rot quickly. Fasten the sides and end boards to bottom boards with angle braces of hot galvanized steel.   57

To make asbestos cement-board benches—the ideal, long-lasting type, impervious to moisture or bacteria—get quarter-inch corrugated asbestos cement-board for the bottoms of the benches and smooth-finished redwood for sides and ends. Sides and ends are fastened in place with steel angle braces. Legs and cross supports are made of pipe. Corrugations (in the asbestos cement-board) running the short way across the bench provide drainage to front or back. Under-bench areas then stay dry and may be used for storage or for additional growing space.

Benches with legs precut to exact length can be ordered from greenhouse manufacturers. If pipe legs are used, split tees are furnished for quick assembly. Wood for sides and bottoms is furnished in random lengths so there will be extra material to allow for waste when benches are cut-to-fit in place. Necessary hardware and fittings are of hot galvanized steel.

If you build your own, make the side benches 2 feet 10 inches wide and the full length of your greenhouse. If your greenhouse is as wide as 14 feet, it will also accommodate a center bench—make this approximately 3 feet 8 inches wide and about 5 feet shorter than the length of your greenhouse to allow space for a walk and a work area at each end. With a supply of pipe on hand, you can also build the pipe legs, a fairly simple job, since split tees make assembly possible without threading of pipe.

At the start, line your wood benches with newspapers or burlap. This prevents soil from falling through the bottom before moisture from watering makes the boards swell enough to close up the spaces. To prevent legs from sinking into the ground (and consequent uneven settling of benches), place a brick or concrete slab footing under each support.

Propagating area

Plan on approximately a 2-foot length of bench space to use for rooting cuttings. If this progagating area is across from your potting area, you can do all your work at one end of the greenhouse. To promote root growth, supply bottom warmth with a soil-heating cable. Unaffected by water, cables come with or without thermostats. Length of the heating cable you buy depends upon the size of the bed. Weave the cable back and forth across the area on a shallow bed of soil or clean sharp mason's sand and cover it with sand. To enclose the propagating area and retain the humidity necessary for successful rooting, fasten a piece of polyethylene or other flexible plastic across the back edge of the bench. Unroll this forward to hang free over the front edge (see Figure 61).

However, if greenhouse space is at a premium, you may want to use all of your bench area to grow plants. Then a seed flat or two filled with clean, sharp sand can serve for propagating plants. To get bottom heat, set the flats above the heater on a shelf supported by brackets.

Work and storage areas

A separate work area about 5 feet wide located at one end of a side bench is a great convenience. This can be just a piece of ¼- or ½-inch Masonite placed on top of an empty bench space, or a more elaborate potting tray consisting of a flat work space with sides and back of ½-inch lumber about 6 to 8 inches high. Here you can pot plants or bulbs, sow seeds and transplant seedlings, even keep records. But if you cannot spare permanent room for these doings, you can let a wide board serve as a portable area. Select a board long enough to reach across the walk from bench to bench. When not in use, it can be placed out of the way under the bench.

Supplies of sand, soil, peatmoss, perhaps firbark, need to be at hand. Bins that can be tilted forward for easy access are fine, built in under the work area, but plastic or metal containers with lids or step-on openers are quite adequate and colorful, too. You can use wooden boxes or nail kegs, or perhaps improvise something from materials at hand. My first "storage bin" was a small old round-topped trunk from the attic which fitted in nicely at the end of the center bench.

The sizes of storage containers depend upon your operations. If you are growing mainly bench plants, you will need extra soil only for an occasional pot plant or bulb-pan, once the benches are filled, and storage containers can be small. However, where you grow mostly pot plants, large storage containers are necessary if adequate supplies are to be available, particularly in winter when bad weather may prevent your obtaining additional materials for late-season transplanting or preparation of flats for early sowing.

22. Note practical arrangement of the work area, and application of shading to protect tuberous begonias.

Shelves

If there is one problem all greenhouse gardeners seem to share, it is the need for more room. Inevitably, enthusiasm outdistances growing space. At the start, the empty greenhouse looks enormous but all too soon it is filled to overflowing. One way to gain more room for potted plants is to put up shelves. Suspend these from the eaves along both sides of an even-span greenhouse or along one side and on the supporting wall of a lean-to. You can hang shelves singly or in double tiers, depending upon the brackets used. They can be shelves of wood—preferably of ⅞-inch thickness to prevent warping in the humid atmosphere—or of glass. Glass is preferred because it cuts off less light from plants in benches below. Also available are attractive, lightweight shelves of perforated aluminum. If necessary, you can install shelves on gable ends of the greenhouse.

Pots

When it comes to choosing between plastic or clay pots, each has advantages and disadvantages. Plastic pots are economical, lightweight, easily cleaned. They come in various attractive colors or clear, and quantities can be stored in a small space. They do not absorb moisture from the soil, as clay pots do, so you do not need to water plants nearly so often.

Clay pots come in one color, brick red. They are heavier than plastic, difficult to keep clean since contact with moist soil encourages algae to form and salts to collect, and they take up a lot of room, but clay does let roots "breathe" through the porous walls. I use both kinds of pots with equal success, but I incline toward clay, especially for large plants, because clay pots provide a more substantial base. If, on a hasty occasion, you water too heavily, clay pots compensate for your error more readily than plastic.

Peat pots, round or square, come in 1½- to 4-inch diameters. Lightweight, easy to handle, they are ideal for use when transplanting seedlings from flats. With peat pots, a second transplanting is unnecessary, for roots grow right through bottom and walls, and some peat pots even contain fertilizer. Since peat pots need not be removed from plants when it is time to transfer to larger quarters or to the garden, growth is not checked as in usual transplanting, and plants receive no setback.

To keep pots of every kind and size handy, store them under benches. If you have a piece of corrugated asbestos cement-board left from your benches, use it below for storage. Nest the pots and lay them in the gulleys of the corrugations where they will stay uniformly in place.

Hanging baskets

For decoration, every greenhouse should have at least one hanging plant—a lantana, a tuberous begonia, or a trailing geranium in luxuriant growth. A galvanized-wire or plastic basket suspended on a wire or chain can be used to display one plant or, filled with sphagnum moss, it can hold several plants of one kind, as tuberous begonias; or different kinds in an attractive combination, as fuchsias with tradescantia and ivy. If you prefer soil to sphagnum, liners of pressed fibers should be used inside the basket frame to contain the soil.

Tools and accessories

At the start, you will probably feel adequately equipped if you have a supply of pots, a flat or two, a length of hose for watering, a trowel, and a pair of scissors. But as your growing operations expand, you will find other items, or different types of what you already have, useful and necessary.

Trowel. I like a flat trowel, the kind used by bricklayers and masons —it was the first type available to me and I learned to use it easily. When potting or transplanting, I draw the flat straight edge across the surface of the potting area, through the soil there and, with a twist of the wrist, flip the trowel full of soil up into the pot. (The usual scoop-type trowel cannot be used this way, and with it the job takes me longer.) With the flat edge, I also mark and press in lines for sowing seeds in flats. I draw the straight edge of the trowel across the soil in a freshly prepared flat, moving it slightly from side to side to form a "drill" or shallow planting space. These guide lines are evenly spaced every 1½ to 2 inches until the whole flat has been marked off.

Dibbles. These round sticks of various sizes, smoothed at one end to fit the palm, pointed at the other end, are fine for making holes in soil where seedlings are to go, in either flats or benches. My own dibble is a rigid, 5-inch-long, hollow plastic tube with rubber cap to protect the palm of my hand, the type florists use on individual flowers for arrangements; a bit unconventional, perhaps, but it was used originally because I didn't have a proper dibble, and I found it so handy I have continued to use it.

Dibble board. A board (the dimensions of the inside of your seed flat) to which a series of dibbles are fastened can be used to mark out the whole transplanting area in one operation. Just put it in place and press down firmly into soil or sand. When you lift it up, a series of evenly spaced holes will have been made.

Tamping block. Almost essential is a piece of wood 4 to 5 inches square for firming soil in freshly filled flats or pots before seeds are sown. You can make a handle for this by fastening a strip of leather on top with space left for fingers to slip underneath, or by fastening an ordinary screen-door handle on top.

Cultivator. This tool, single or double pronged, with wood or plastic handle, is used to aerate soil and get rid of weeds between plants in

23. Cheesecloth suspended inside this greenhouse furnishes just the right amount of shading for camellias. (ROCHE PHOTO)

bench rows or lines of pots. You can easily make such a tool: bend an 18-inch length of fairly heavy galvanized wire in half and twist the pieces together for about 6 inches below the bend—this makes a handle. Separate the two pieces of wire and bend them at right angles to the handle for the next half-inch, again at right angles for an inch, and then bend the last 1½ inches of each piece downward. Wrap the 6-inch twisted handle with masking tape for comfortable handling.

Watering can. Select a type with a 12-inch or longer narrow spout, equipped with a removable rose (a perforated sprinkler cap for distributing water in a very fine spray). The rose in place at the end of the spout is ideal for watering seedlings and small transplanted plants. With the rose removed, the long spout reaches to pots and flats on high shelves without splashing plants in benches below. Don't get too large a watering can, no larger, say, than 1½ to 2 gallon capacity. The large ones are light when empty, but when filled with water they are heavy and unwieldy when you must raise them above shoulder height to water shelf plants.

Hose. for general watering, ½- or ⅝-inch diameter garden hose long enough to reach all areas of the greenhouse is essential; a spray nozzle for the hose is very useful.

Rubber-bulb hand sprayer. Buy a large size with a fine spray-head for misting cuttings and seedlings, orchids, and other humidity-loving plants.

Scoop. A good-sized one is useful for transferring soil from bins or containers to potting bench, for filling large pots and flats, and for measuring proportions when you are preparing quantities of special soil mixtures. A metal funnel with the spout corked or the handled half of a liquid bleach bottle make inexpensive scoops.

Sieves. To fill benches with garden soil or to mix a batch of potting soil, you need sieves to screen out stones and twigs. If you want only a small amount of soil to pot a few plants, a standard round kitchen strainer will do. For sifting a larger quantity of soil, make a sieve by tacking a piece of ½-inch-mesh galvanized or aluminum wire to a wooden frame, the size determined by ease of handling. Sieves for small amounts of soil should use ¼-inch-mesh wire.

Cane or bamboo stakes. Buy these in bundles for use as supports for tall plants, or to hold up wires or strings when you are making temporary frame supports for benched plants.

Green cord. A ball or two is useful for making criss-cross supports between bamboo or cane stakes that support carnations or snapdragons.

Plant ties. You can fasten plants to stakes with bits of string or raffia if you wish, but commercial plant ties make the chore much easier. These inexpensive dark-green pieces of pliable paper-covered wire come in boxes of different lengths or in more economical rolls. With these plant ties, it takes only a moment to fasten a tall plant to a stake or a vigorous vine to a wall nail, and the ties are practically invisible.

Plant tags. It is a good idea to mark plants for identification. Use a simple name tag to help you get to know them, or obtain large labels slanted at the top for easy reading. The surface is sufficiently large to write name, date of planting, and abbreviated cultural directions for easy reference on unfamiliar plants—especially valuable if you grow a variety of plants.

Scissors. Get a pair of good nickel-plated hot-drop forged steel, 7 to

7½ inches long, for cutting flower stems, seed packets, string. If you are wise, you will hide these from all but yourself; otherwise they are bound to disappear to be used for purposes other than gardening.

Sharp knife. Tuck this away, too, so you will have it when you need it for separating side shoots from main stems, cutting tubers for propagating, or making cuttings of plants.

Aerosol spray. Keep a can on hand for quick spot-control of insects when you haven't time to do a thorough spraying job. A cardboard "pop-gun" type duster similar to outdoor garden dusters also has emergency value for treatment of insects or disease.

Cotton swabs and alcohol. Keep these on hand for early and immediate control of mealy bugs.

Improvised items. Many other greenhouse aids can easily be improvised. Coat hangers, straightened out or bent, make excellent pot or basket hangers, plant stakes, or cultivators. Large plastic boxes with covers make good propagating boxes; plastic sandwich boxes can be used as pot saucers; coffee cans or small jars provide safe storage for seeds; well-washed bottles that contained window-cleaning spray can be filled with clear water for misting plants; water-filled peanut-butter jars are fine for rooting wax begonia cuttings. Just use your imagination, adapt, and have fun at no expense!

5

Soils and Fertilizers

The subject of soils, soil mixtures, and fertilizers has been made far too complex and mysterious. At the start, there are only a few things you need to know. You will learn by *doing*, and more easily than by *reading*. Soil has two functions—to support plants and to nourish them —and fertilizers or plant foods contribute to this second essential function.

SOILS

In a greenhouse you soon discover how to vary the soil elements— you supply the fine-rooted African-violets with a fairly light mixture, geraniums and amaryllis with something more substantial. You discover that pH isn't all that peculiar and that, anyway, most plants are amazingly accommodating to variations in soil from acid to alkaline. Many different kinds of plants thrive on just about the same well-balanced soil mixture and on somewhat the same fertilizers. Soils are nothing to get alarmed about, but they are a fascinating study. As you come to know more about the culture of your favorite plants, you are also bound to find out a lot about soils. The soil that comes directly from your yard or garden does not necessarily contain the minerals and other elements that encourage growth in all types of plants in a greenhouse. So you may want to prepare a good growing mixture by making some additions. But first, consider the structure of the soil you have.

67

Texture of soil

The consistency of soil is as important as its fertility, so before you add plant foods, try to develop a soil mixture of good texture, a soil in which moisture is retained long enough to benefit roots but not so long as to rot them. If the soil mixture is too thin, water runs through too fast for plants to benefit; if it is too heavy and always wet, oxygen cannot reach roots. In the intricate process of food production, oxygen and moisture in the soil, carbon dioxide in the air, along with sunlight, operate in conjunction with the green coloring (cholorophyll) in the leaves to change food elements into forms that plants can assimilate.

Loam from a well-worked flower bed may have fairly good consistency, for loam is composed of clay, sand, and organic matter, their proportions depending on where you live.

Organic matter is material that was once living, as leafmold or other decayed vegetation, manure, or peatmoss. Very-well-rotted leaves are an invaluable source; you may even put them through a coarse sieve for easier handling. You may already have a compost pile where in the fall you heap up leaves with or without layers of soil or sod between. Even a small compost pile is useful, and leaves retained long enough in a wire circle behind a big forsythia bush are bound to rot; these can be an excellent and easy source of organic material in which beneficial bacteria develop—another factor in the good growth of plants.

Manure is a source of organic material, but scarce today in the fresh form. If you can obtain this, do not use it until it is well rotted, which takes at least six months. With fresh manure, there is danger of burning roots of plants. Readily available is dehydrated manure sold in bags. This can be used at once to improve the consistency of soil.

Then there are the various peatmosses—long-decayed plants from bogs or swamps. Peatmoss offers an excellent means of retaining moisture in a soil mixture.

Sand has an opposite use, and I refer to builder's or mason's sand, not the seashore type. Sand loosens soil to allow proper drainage after the water-holding elements present have performed their function. In heavy or sticky soils, sand is a vital ingredient, for it separates the clay particles; more sand is required with heavy clay than in a light open soil. There are also a number of sterile commercial preparations like perlite or vermiculite that are as good as sand to lighten soils.

Clay is the mineral-rich element in soil, essential to your mixture in the proper proportions.

With these essential elements, then, you can produce soil mixtures to suit most plants and, if your garden loam is particularly fertile, extra plant food may not be needed. There are bound to be some nutrients in the various organic materials you use, though not a great deal. However, many a handsome plant has grown and bloomed in the old "equal-thirds" mixture, suggested here for general use:

> 1 part garden loam
> 1 part leafmold (or other organic material)
> 1 part sharp, clean, builder's sand

A modification of the above is better for plants that require much moisture but good drainage:

> 1 part garden loam
> 1 part peatmoss
> 1 part leafmold
> 1 part sharp, clean, builder's sand

For plants that definitely require an acid soil, use:

> 1 part garden loam
> 2 parts leafmold or peatmoss
> 1 part well-rotted or dehydrated cow manure
> 1 part sharp, clean, builder's sand

Sterilizing your garden soil

If you use your own garden soil for pot or bench plants, it may be wise to sterilize it to get rid of harmful bacteria, insects, and weed seeds. You can do this in your kitchen oven if you can stand a pungent, earthy smell for a day or so. Here is the way it works: fill a large roaster pan or preserving kettle with garden soil, cover with aluminum foil pricked in many places to let steam escape, and bake for half to three-quarters of an hour at about 180 F. Repeat the process until the required amount has been sterilized. Let cool completely and stir it well before you use it.

My first greenhouse plantings were made in soil sterilized in this way, but I admit that subsequently I have used soil taken directly from the garden without sterilizing it, and results were just as good.

(However, I did live in an apparently nematode-free area.) Late in spring as plants were removed to make way for new plantings or early in summer at the end of the growing season, I turned over the soil in the benches, mixed in an all-purpose fertilizer, some clean sharp sand, and a little peatmoss or unmilled sphagnum moss, even osmunda fiber —whatever I happened to have on hand. A few weeds may appear in this mixture, but they are easily pulled and hardly a problem. Preparation of soil can be as simple and routine as mine, making your greenhouse gardening easier and more enjoyable, or you can purchase the soil you need.

Buying sterilized soil mixtures

An easy way—particularly if you are not too experienced with plants —is to buy packaged soil or a readymade loose mixture from your garden center or florist. In some neighborhoods, you can get bags of convenient size, and even specific mixtures prepared for various types of plants. (However, commercial combinations bought in hardware stores have not been invariably satisfactory; often they are very light, and those available are not sufficiently labeled for various plants.) If your work or storage area is limited—or your time—you may find it convenient to buy quite small amounts according to your needs. From my own experience this is most satisfactory and, incidentally, I almost never have to add anything to the basic mixture I select at our fine garden center. Furthermore, most packaged soils or those from florists are already sterilized, and this is a real advantage.

But you may prefer to be more scientific about soil in order to bring to perfection some one group of plants. If so, get in touch with your county agricultural agent or state college horticultural department. From either you can get the latest information on soil preparation for the plants of your particular interest. You can also buy a soil-testing kit to get the pH reading of the soil you have, and then improve it according to the advice given. In some states, at no cost or for a small fee, your county agent will test your soil for you.

FERTILIZERS

Fertilizers or plant foods, also referred to as nutrients, are materials added to the soil to stimulate plant growth and produce flowers. Many "good" soils are already rich in the necessary elements, but when soil is used over and over again and constant production is expected, soil must be continuously amended. For best results three major elements—nitrogen, phosphorus, and potassium—must always be present in soil in correct proportions. Fertilizer manufacturers list these three main elements on packages and cans in a numerical ratio in the order given above, as 4-12-4 or 5-10-5. Thus, a 4-12-4 fertilizer contains 4 per cent nitrogen, 12 per cent phosphorus, and 4 per cent potassium. (Sometimes there is a statement as to how much of the nitrogen is from organic sources.) Inert or filler material makes up the amount to 100 per cent.

Nitrogen stimulates growth, strengthens stems, and promotes healthy green foliage. Weak, stunted or spindly growth and yellow-green leaf color *usually* indicate a lack of nitrogen. An oversupply of nitrogen results in soft lush leaves, few flowers, and susceptibility to disease.

Phosphorus is also a stimulant; it promotes root growth and encourages flower and seed production. If too little phosphorus is available, plants incline to shed lower leaves and yellow edges develop on those that remain. Plants get sappy and require more staking than usual when soil lacks phosphorus.

Potassium or potash builds up resistance to disease. It stabilizes growth, improves plant and flower color, and increases productivity. A dull-looking plant usually lacks potassium, but too much potassium causes weak growth that cannot support itself. Mottled foliage also indicates lack of potassium—lower leaves are affected first, and yellow edges progress to brown until the whole leaf is affected.

Then there are the various trace elements—iron, boron, manganese, and others—which in minute quantities are important to healthy plant life. The commercial "all-purpose" plant foods contain the necessary trace elements, so unless you want to go into the matter rather thoroughly, just rely on them, changing brands occasionally to take advantage of the different emphasis of elements in the different formulas, and do follow the manufacturer's directions for mixing and applying.

How and when to fertilize

Never apply fertilizer to dry soil. When soil is parched, even dilute solutions of fertilizer may be strong enough to burn roots. If your plants are dry and it is a convenient time for you to feed them, give a light, quick watering before you prepare the fertilizer. Moisture will have penetrated to roots while you are mixing the solution, and trouble will be avoided.

Some gardeners give weak solutions of fertilizer as soon as seedlings show the first true leaves and gradually increase the strength according to the manufacturer's directions. I prefer to wait until seedlings have been transplanted and perk up on their own. I find the soil they are sown in is usually adequate to start them into vigorous growth. However, if you sow seeds in sphagnum moss or in one of the sterile mediums like perlite or vermiculite that contain no nutrients, by all means give a first light feeding as soon as seeds germinate.

On mature plants I have used both dry and liquid fertilizers. At present, I am partial to fish oil emulsion. I mix it with water, and use it as a general fertilizer—everything in the greenhouse gets it, and everything seems to thrive on it.

It is a good idea to establish a schedule for fertilizing. Every two weeks during periods of active growth is the usual recommendation. If this is not convenient, don't be alarmed. Most plants will thrive with less frequent and less regular applications.

While it is true that certain nutrients are necessary and beneficial, it is also true that overfertilizing can be harmful to plants. Keep an eye on the reactions of your plants to fertilizer. When they want to rest, let them, as during stretches of dull weather. When they show signs of new life, particularly in sunny weather in late winter and early spring, encourage them with the recommended fortnightly feedings.

6

A Clean and Healthy Greenhouse

The greenhouse gardener must attend to three equally important matters if he is to have healthy, pest-free, disease-free plants, and he must be alert to all three matters at all times and continuously: *environment, good housekeeping,* and *preventive control of pests and diseases.*

ENVIRONMENT
The first important step is to maintain a healthy physical environment for plants. Pay particular attention to watering, control of temperature, ventilation, sanitary working conditions, introduction of new plants to the greenhouse, and safe storage of chemicals.

Watering. It is impossible to specify hard-and-fast rules about watering greenhouse plants because the plants vary in their water requirement. The general recommendations are: water when temperature is rising (usually before noon); try to avoid watering on dull, cloudy days; try not to let moisture remain on foliage overnight when greenhouse temperature is lower; and do not overwater. These matters are explained in detail in Chapter 3. Although you cannot *always* follow the recommendations and rules, and sometimes it is not essential for you to do so, it is beneficial to keep them in mind.

Temperature control. Fluctuations of temperature should be avoided. If at all possible, control the heat and ventilation in your greenhouse automatically. Set the heat thermostat for the night temperature you wish to maintain, set the ventilation thermostat 10 degrees higher than

73

the heat thermostat—and then let them alone. When I started green-house gardening, I was told that the daytime temperature should be 10 to 20 degrees higher than the minimum maintained at night, so every morning I raised the setting on the heat thermostat and every evening I returned it to its nighttime setting. Obviously, this was un-necessary—the sun automatically takes care of the extra heat during the day; and anyway, if the sun does not shine, plant growth is slowed and plants do better without the extra heat.

Ventilation. Fresh air is extremely important in winter as well as in summer. Take care to avoid unnecessary drafts, but admit some fresh air to the greenhouse daily, though not so frequently and for shorter periods of time during winter. The limit control on most ventilation units can be set to permit partial opening of vents during winter weather.

Plant diseases and pests thrive in a warm, closed, humid atmosphere. If the greenhouse is well ventilated and air circulation around plants is maintained, few problems of this nature should be encountered. Avoid crowding your plants—space them sufficiently far apart in flats or benches to permit air to circulate around them, and leave space around each potted plant for the same reason.

Sanitary working conditions. Use sterilized planting mediums, keep work areas spotless and hands and equipment clean. Remove fading or deteriorating flowers and leaves from plants. Do not accumulate dis-carded leaves and blossoms—destroy them immediately, preferably by burning, if there has been any evidence of disease. Sterilize cutting tools —knife blades or scissors can be passed through a match or gas flame easily to provide a quick means of sterilization.

Gift plants. A clean-looking gift plant often harbors unhatched pests. As a precautionary measure, isolate or "put on probation" for at least three weeks all gift or newly purchased plants and cuttings before placing them near or among your other plants. Even if, at the end of three to four weeks, you see no evidence of pests or disease on the new acquisitions, dust or spray with pesticide before allowing them to join the plant community.

Safe storage of chemicals. Chemicals used in pesticides, fungicides, and fertilizers may be poisonous to humans and animals, and these materials should be stored in a convenient but safe area, preferably under lock and key, so they are accessible only to the knowedgeable gardener for his own use.

GOOD HOUSEKEEPING

Every experienced greenhouse gardener has learned that good housekeeping is essential to healthy, happy plants and flowers. Yet, the most careful among us find an unbelievable accumulation of odds and ends and bits and pieces of just about everything imaginable working its way into every nook and cranny not occupied by plants.

Cleanliness must be practiced daily. It must become an automatic part of the greenhouse operation; it must be a routine that you establish on the first day your greenhouse is put into operation and continue for as long as you have a greenhouse. Insects rarely reproduce and diseases rarely spread in a greenhouse that starts clean and stays that way. As you progress into the various phases of under-glass gardening, you will be glad that you developed the cleanliness habit right from the start.

Whether you are starting in a spotless new greenhouse or are an old hand at the gardening game who already follows the summer cleanup outlined later, try not to let planting and growing activities overwhelm you to the point of forgetting to be a tidy housekeeper.

Daily housekeeping and maintenance

Take a minute or two to plan each greenhouse activity. Collect the necessary materials: pots, flats, planting medium, seeds, bulbs, all the tools you will need. The actual work of planting, transplanting, or maintenance will go smoothly, efficiently and tidily if confusion is anticipated and avoided. Stopping in the middle of a job to procure a necessary tool or material encourages haste; haste causes spills, upsets, and laxness of attention to good planting procedures. Good intentions never seem to clean up the spilled and upset materials; one or two such incidents and you no longer have a spotlessly clean greenhouse. Occasionally an accident will occur. Broken crock or soil spilled in the work area is easily retrieved. Anything spilled that is not reusable, as liquid fertilizer, water, or rooting powders, should be soaked or brushed up and disposed of in a covered trash can kept conveniently under the bench for just this purpose.

To dispose of old soil or bark preparatory to repotting, to trim dead roots, or to remove foliage, hold the plant or cutting over the trash receptacle as you work and avoid an accumulation of debris in the work area.

When you have finished a job, put away the unused materials, clean the tools, and empty the trash container. It is easier to handle half-empty receptacles than to lift and carry away those filled to overflowing, the contents of which, incidentally, may already be at work producing or reproducing pests and diseases.

Next to refilling benches with fresh soil, I think the dirtiest and least interesting chore in your greenhouse will be the cleaning of used flower pots. You will never be without a certain number of pots to be cleaned (even plastic ones must be washed, though they do not require wire-brushing to remove accumulations of algae and crusted salts), but these should not be allowed to accumulate in number to the point that you are faced with a large, time-consuming, dirty chore. When you know you will be in the greenhouse for an hour or two, use the first few moments to prepare a solution of Lysol, water softener and water, and place the dirty pots to soak. When your scheduled work is completed, it will be a simple matter to wisk the soaked clay pots with a wire brush or wipe off the plastic pots. A quick rinse in clear water, and a supply of clean pots will always be ready. A commercial product, Algae-Go, lightens the pot-cleaning chore considerably and lessens a natural inclination to let dirty empty pots accumulate.

Increased daylength and more frequent watering during the spring growing season promotes growth of weeds. Check under-bench areas frequently, bench soil and pots, too. At the first sign of weeds, dig out—do not pull up—these pesky little growers. Most weeds develop tremendous root systems; if they are not removed quickly, you are bound to leave broken-off roots in the soil which will produce new plantlets and a never-ending battle will ensue.

Thorough summer housecleaning

At least one major cleanup should be scheduled for the greenhouse each year, and the ideal time for this is during the summer, when the growing schedule is at a low point or the greenhouse has been emptied by moving pot plants and baskets into the cool shade of the outdoor garden. If some of your plants require year-round greenhouse protection, it is still possible to move them outdoors for a single day without harmful results if you choose the day carefully—avoid strong winds or possible showers, and shelter the plants under bushes or trees to prevent sunburn.

Start the greenhouse cleaning by removing unwashed pots and flats that have found their way under the benches. Store them outside temporarily and concentrate on the interior cleanup. Next, collect all the bottles, boxes, and cans of pesticides, fungicides, and fertilizers, place them carefully in a labeled carton, and store the carton out of the reach of children and pets. If you have small quantities of soil, sand, and other potting materials, remove these also. If your materials are contained in a permanent arrangement of large containers, they may be left in place, but cover them tightly.

If the bench soil must be replaced, empty the benches at this point. Benches of asbestos cement-board should be hosed to remove all particles of soil; it may be necessary to scrub wood benches with a wire brush to remove accumulations of soil. While the benches are empty, wash all glass on the inside with a long-handled brush or sponge. One of the extension-rod car-washing brushes that attaches to the end of a hose will do a very satisfactory job with little effort. Do not neglect the roof glass, though most of the accumulated soil, algae, and grime will be at bench height (and on the glass below benches if your greenhouse has glass to the ground).

Wood-framed greenhouses in need of painting should receive at least one coat of paint on the inside and two coats on the outside to protect them from weather, but the structure must be thoroughly dry before the paint is applied. Use only paint specially recommended for greenhouse use. Any structural parts of steel should be wire-brushed and given a coat of rust-preventive paint. Aluminum-framed structures do not need painting or wire-brushing, as the aluminum used for greenhouses is anodized and maintenance-free.

Motors that operate ventilating and heating equipment should be checked and instructions for their particular care referred to. The heating system should receive its annual inspection and cleaning. Test all thermostats, humidistats, and temperature-alarm systems; check thermometers and hygrometers for accuracy. Replace broken or cracked glass; if your house is putty-glazed, inspect the glazing for voids caused by drying and re-putty where necessary.

If your greenhouse has a dirt or a gravel floor, you will probably have a fine crop of weeds growing in corners or around bench legs. Dig the weeds out with a trowel or small shovel, being sure to get the roots.

New soil for benches should be sterilized, either before it is brought into the greenhouse or after it has been placed in the benches. Use a specially built sterilizing pit or one of the commercial sterilizing preparations manufactured for this purpose. Fumigate and spray the interior ("how-to" instructions for fumigating and spraying appear at the end of this chapter), and you are ready to restock your greenhouse.

Return only *clean* pots, flats, and other materials and supplies to your scrubbed, repaired greenhouse. Put the pesticides, fungicides, fertilizers and other chemicals in their proper safe location, and store tools and equipment where they belong.

If plants have been summering outdoors, inspect them carefully—tops, sides, and bottoms of pots *and* plants—for slugs and snails, and spray plants to eliminate aphids, red spiders, or mealy bugs. Do this work outdoors before returning the plants to your clean greenhouse.

This cleanup program, if planned and carried out systematically, requires very little time. Your gardening activities will be more pleasant and results will be more satisfactory because of this small time and effort taken from your summer funtime.

PREVENTIVE CONTROL OF PESTS AND DISEASES

If you plan your growing operation for one temperature range, and if you specialize in one or two—or at most, several—types of plants and flowers, you will automatically reduce to a minimum the number and kinds of pests and diseases that you might encounter if you grew many different kinds of plants with quite different cultural requirements.

It is easier to prevent trouble than to cure it. A program of prevention should be part of the regular operating routine of your greenhouse. To establish such a program, you should know something about the various insects and diseases that might be troublesome, though it is not likely that any one greenhouse could be plagued by *all* of the afflictions that will be mentioned below. While these are by no means all the kinds of pests and diseases that affect plant growth, they are the ones that hobby gardeners will most likely encounter at one time or another.

Investigate the various insecticides, miticides, fungicides, and general pesticides available before you start your gardening program, and keep informed of new ones as they are marketed. For your preventive program, select one or two that you feel you can use with confidence. Some plants are adversely affected by certain chemicals, so particular attention should be paid to each manufacturer's instructions about how and where to use his product. Orchid blossoms, especially, are easily spotted, and sprayed materials should not be used in their immediate vicinity.

Pests

There are three general classifications of pests: chewing, sucking, and rasping.

Chewing pests, as ants, cutworms, leaf rollers, and leaf tiers, though not so prevalent as some others, do considerable damage by chewing seedlings, cutting off stems and foliage, and destroying flowers. Ants themselves do little damage to plants, but they carry aphids and mealy bugs from plant to plant throughout the greenhouse. Since chewing pests feed on *foliage,* they are most easily controlled by poisons applied to the areas of the plant on which they feed—"stomach" poisons which the pests consume along with the greenery.

Sucking pests, as aphids, cyclamen mites, white flies, mealy bugs, and red spiders, pierce the foliage, generally from the underside, to suck the *juices* from inside leaves and stems. Control is accomplished by spraying "contact" poisons directly on the pests.

Rasping pests, as thrips, rasp the foliage to obtain the *juices* from the injured section. These, too, are controlled by "contact" poisons sprayed directly on the pests.

Treatment must continue

The life cycles of these various pests differ greatly, and preventive or control measures must be taken accordingly. Aphids, which produce live young, have a life cycle of about 25 to 30 days during which time a female may reproduce several groups of 30 or more; a majority of the young will be females that will be mature enough in 10 to 12 days to

produce another generation. The female red spider lays as many as 8
eggs daily; these hatch in 5 days and, depending on the temperature in
the greenhouse, will produce another generation in from 10 days to a
couple of months.

Obviously, then, one treatment is not sufficient to destroy any particular pest infestation. Repeated treatments over a period of at least
a month (once every ten days) are necessary to assure the destruction
of not only the breeding generation but also of those maturing later
and those still in the incubation period.

Pest immunity to chemicals

Another aspect of pest eradication is that some pests develop an
immunity to certain sprays or dusts, either in the present generation
or in succeeding generations hatched from eggs that have been subjected to treatment. When immunity is established, some different
pesticide will have to be tried, and this is where up-to-the-minute information will serve you well.

Up-to-date bulletins

College research departments, agricultural experiment stations, and
chemical companies have spent and continue to spend much time and
money to research the habits of various pests that plague greenhouse
plants and to develop controlling sprays and dusts. Most of these
organizations publish bulletins (available to you for the asking or for
a very small fee) that furnish valuable, up-to-the-minute information.

Recognizing the pests

The important thing in controlling and eradicating greenhouse pests
is to recognize them quickly so the proper treatment may be started
without delay. These descriptions may be helpful:

Aphids may be yellow, green, or black. They are minute in size, with
plump bodies, some winged and others not. They are usually found
on new, tender shoots and leaves, and when aphids are present leaves
will soon become distorted.

Cyclamen mites are invisible to the naked eye. Infestation should be
suspected if new growth is distorted or twisted and new leaves become
progressively smaller, or growth appears to stop.

Leaf tiers are small green or bronze caterpillars that spin webs around leaves, causing the edges of the leaves to roll under. These pests are sometimes called leaf rollers.

Mealy bugs look like dabs of fuzzy white cotton at the onset, later developing an oval shape with tiny pointed appendages. The cottony coating has a waxy texture that is difficult to penetrate.

Nematodes (foliar) attack the leaves, leaving brown spots which are clearly visible. Wetting the foliage may encourage spread of this pest.

Nematodes (root-knot) are tiny eel worms that irritate roots in which they hatch and form knots or galls wherever tissue is injured. They especially attack African-violets, begonias, cyclamens, and chrysanthemums. Growth is seriously affected, and plants become stunted or deformed. Steam sterilization of soil is an effective control.

Red-spider mites are troublesome pests, since they are so small they cannot be seen without a magnifying glass. They usually attack the underside of tender new growth which becomes mottled, and turns brown and dies if the infestation is heavy. You will notice a fine web, which may eventually envelop the entire plant. This pest thrives in a dry atmosphere, so a fine water misting, spraying, or washing of susceptible plants is recommended.

Scales are small white or brown sucking insects that hide themselves under a hard protective covering that looks like a dried oval scab.

Snails and *slugs* may be a bit troublesome if you grow orchids or other plants that require high humidity. Plants that are moved outdoors for the summer sometimes acquire these pests. Before returning plants to the greenhouse, inspect pots carefully and flick out with a small stick and destroy any slugs or snails you find. In my many years of orchid growing I have been troubled only once with this problem. The pests were picked up in the outdoor garden, but a careful inspection revealed them before the pots were returned to the benches in the greenhouse.

Thrips are thin, winged when adult, and can be tan, yellow, brown, or black. They are difficult to detect when small, but affected foliage has a silvery appearance, and flower petals are streaked or deformed.

White flies, minute in size, are aptly named. If a plant infested with this pest is disturbed, a cloud of hundreds of tiny white flies are visible as they fly from the undersides of the leaves, leaving behind countless tiny eggs that keep developing.

Diseases

As might be supposed, pests traveling from one plant to another can spread diseases, so by controlling the pests you simultaneously safeguard your greenhouse from certain diseases of plants. Here are descriptions of the most common diseases in greenhouses:

Damp-off is the most common of the fungous diseases, and the one most likely to be encountered first by the home gardener. It attacks seedlings particularly, and is evident when healthy plants suddenly rot off at the soil line. Sterilized planting mediums have pretty well brought damp-off under control, but if you must use unsterilized soil for planting seeds, you will do well to drench it first with a fungicide, such as Pano-Drench.

Leaf-spot causes purple, brown, or black spots on the foliage. Many of the favorite plants of the hobby gardener are susceptible: roses, caranations, cyclamens, and other flowering plants. Leaf-spot is spread from one plant to another by splashing water on foliage. Spraying or dusting with ferban (Fermate) will help to control this problem. Infected foliage and blossoms should be removed from the plant and destroyed, preferably by burning.

Mildew appears on leaves and stems as powdery white areas, and affects both upper and lower leaf surfaces. The spores of powdery mildew are transported through the air when the relative humidity is extremely high. Dusting with sulfur is usually effective, but proper air circulation must be maintained.

Rot (*stem* and *root*) attacks plants at the surface or just below the surface of the soil. The fungus that causes this troublesome problem may travel through the soil from an infected plant to healthy ones. Soil drenches will prevent the disease from traveling to healthy plants, but those already affected must be destroyed, as there is no known cure.

Rust appears on snapdragons and carnations especially, in blister-like areas which, when broken, spew forth a rusty-looking powdery substance that is spread to unaffected areas by air currents or water splashed on the foliage. A dusting of Fermate will prevent development of the spores.

Aerosol sprays

While there are numerous pests and diseases to which plants are susceptible, the hobby gardener will probably have only one or two to contend with, according to the kinds of plants he grows. Sprays or dusts applied in a greenhouse remain effective for a longer period than they do outdoors as they are not washed away by rain or blown away by brisk winds. Aerosol sprays are effective in small hobby greenhouses, say 10 by 10 feet or so, and the convenience of not having to mix several ingredients to make an effective pesticide is a boon to the amateur gardener. Aerosol cans may seem to be expensive, but several applications would stretch the cost over a period of time, and the convenience is well worth the few extra pennies. When the greenhouse is closed up for the night, a quick spray with an aerosol usually provides adequate control or prevention, and no time is lost from the growing schedule.

Systemic poisons

A radical change in control of insects and diseases is being effected with the development of the new systemic poisons. These are applied to the soil and assimilated by the plant throughout its entire structure in quantities sufficient to kill insects and destroy bacteria and fungi. Chewing and sucking pests can be effectively controlled with systemics for periods of several weeks with one or two applications. Most systemics are extremely toxic to humans and animals, and the amateur gardener must handle them with respect and caution. Professional growers have access to several systemics, but amateurs should confine themselves to Cygon 267 or Scope, and never re-use the containers. Such are the advances being made in this field, however, that other systemics may be available for general use soon.

Spraying

Be sure to spray the undersides of foliage as well as the upper surfaces, because some pests prefer the hidden areas. A small amount of soap or detergent powder added to most spray solutions acts as a "spreader" to insure complete saturation and adherence. Sprays and dusts contain chemical elements which in some instances are incompatible, so thoroughly clean your spraying equipment after each use, and don't use the same equipment for sprays as for fertilizers. Prepare only enough spraying solution to take care of your immediate needs; throw out any that is left over. An amateur gardener should *especially* avoid using parathion.

CAUTION: If your greenhouse is attached to your home, be sure the spray material is one that will not penetrate cracks or other openings between house and greenhouse. When you are ready to spray or dust, post a "No Admittance" sign on the greenhouse door—face the sign to the outside to warn anyone approaching the greenhouse, but hang it on the *inside* of the glass door so it won't be knocked off or blown away. Close the ventilators to contain the spray or dust in contact with plants. Wear a mask or respirator if it is recommended for the product you are using. Start the operation at the end of the greenhouse opposite the door, and work toward the door so you can step outside and close and lock the greenhouse door immediately.

Fumigating

A smoke generator (*not* a bomb) is the only fumigator recommended for use in a hobby greenhouse; the generated smoke carries the pesticide to every part of the greenhouse, insuring complete coverage and providing treatment for most of the pests likely to appear in a home greenhouse. Two fumigators recommended are Plantfume 103 for greenhouses of 5,000 cubic feet or larger; and Fulex Smoke Generators, which come in sizes suitable for small greenhouses, as 1,000 cubic feet or 2,000 cubic feet. Fulex Smoke Generators can be divided safely, to take care of even smaller areas, whereas Plantfume 103 cannot be thus reduced. Other fumigators available to commercial greenhouse operators should not be used by amateur growers.

Fumigate on a regular schedule as a preventive measure.

CAUTION: Follow the manufacturer's directions exactly. Post a conspicuous "No Admittance" sign where it cannot be blown away or removed, close the ventilators, and be prepared to step outside and close and lock the greenhouse door the instant you activate the smoke generator.

CAUTION: No kind of fumigator, including smoke generators, should be used in a greenhouse attached to a residence or other building that houses people or animals, as the smoke penetrates even the most minute crack or opening.

7

Dress up Your Garden
Under Glass

A greenhouse filled with flowering plants, the atmosphere pleasant with the scent of green growth and fragrant bloom, is always attractive. But there are some easy ways to make it even prettier, and if you plan to use part of it as an extension of your living room, perhaps as a dining area or just a place with chairs where you can rest occasionally, you will treat that section in a special way.

The hobby greenhouse of today is a far cry from its prototype, the old-fashioned stovehouse which was used mainly to winter-over tender decorative plants or to grow tropical citrus and other fruits. Now, a greenhouse makes possible not only a colorful year-round garden but it may be a means to health and an escape from the turmoil of business; it may become a family-room or a place for entertaining . . . and always for fun. No longer a luxury but a possibility for most home owners, the modern greenhouse serves your own particular purpose.

Dressing up the outside

The structure itself is more attractive if it appears to be a part of your home instead of an afterthought. This is true particularly of lean-to greenhouses, which are so inviting when they have the look of an extra room. And if these are lighted at night, how lovely the flowers look from within and from without. Greenhouse foundations of concrete or other solid material can be painted to match your house, roll-up shades of wood can be treated in the same manner. When you

85

24. The straight-eave lean-to greenhouse (above) extends the living area of the home.

shade your greenhouse from the sun, shade it with the light-green flexible plastic film suggested in Chapter 3 instead of with streaked, painted-on shading compound. The outside area around the greenhouse can be landscaped or planted with low evergreen shrubs or flowering plants.

Decorating the functional greenhouse

If your garden under glass is mainly functional, that is, a place only for the growing of plants, it can still be a picture if several attractive hanging baskets planted with colorful plants—lavender and yellow lantanas or shocking-pink ivy-leaved geraniums, perhaps—are nicely spaced and suspended from the roof bar. For baskets you might select trailing foliage plants: big chlorophytums; a collection of ivies with large or small green or variegated leaves; a collection of peperomias; maybe geranium species, like sprawling peppermint-scented *Pelargonium tomentosum,* that fill the greenhouse with tantalizing herbal aromas when the sun shines on them. A well-grown basket plant attracts the eye every time.

On glass shelves, pots of trailing plants soften the rigid lines of greenhouse structure and straight benches. Here is a place for wax-plants, trailers like Begonia 'Limminghei', and gesneriads such as hypocyrtas and columneas that bloom and bloom. On shelves, you can place interesting ceramic containers in colors that will not compete with plants. In these, dish gardens can be arranged to be brought into the house for occasional decoration there. A shelf is also a good place to show off pots of brilliant blue lobelia or pink or white clouds of baby's-breath, or cascades of bright yellow, salmon, orange, and red nasturtiums. (Many other trailing plants suitable for baskets or shelves are suggested in Chapter 11.)

Perhaps it is imaginative planting of the edges of the benches that does the most to make the functional greenhouse attractive. In long lines, trailing white and lavender sweet-alyssum blooms throughout the year if it is sheared back now and then, or miniature ivies are permanently green and graceful.

If you grow mostly potted plants, spread pebbles over the benches instead of soil; the white ones, sometimes called roofing pebbles, look best.

The housewall of a lean-to greenhouse has infinite possibilities for growing plants decoratively. Here you can attach tiers of metal trays from ridge to ground, to hold plants that form a living wall of greenery. I have seen them filled with asparagus fern (*Asparagus Sprengeri*), always a riotous grower. Here, too, is a place for handsomely designed wrought-iron brackets to hold one or many trailing plants, and there are brass plaques, ceramic figures, and lavaboes to fasten among the trailing plants.

To minimize the utilitarian appearance of the dirt floor of a greenhouse, make a walk of brick, perhaps laid in an interesting pattern, with no cement of course, but on a 3- to 4-inch layer of clean, washed, gravel-free sand. Or use evenly cut and evenly spaced pieces of flagstones, also laid on sand. A slat walk of natural wood that has been treated with a preservative looks well and keeps your feet dry; you

25. The curved-eave lean-to (above) converts a flagstone patio to a pleasant garden room.

can let it weather naturally or cover it with gray or green deck paint instead of the preservative.

A small pool, fountain, or waterfall with recirculating water adds a great deal of interest to a greenhouse, furnishes some air moisture, and provides a place to grow a few of the beautiful plants that grow only in water.

Greenhouse living room

The lean-to greenhouse attached to living- or dining-room, study, kitchen, or bedroom, and planned for living like other rooms in the house as well as for the cultivation of plants, can be made more attractive by a certain amount of concealment. If you have standard benches on either side and plan to use the center area or one end of the greenhouse for a family area, hide the under-bench storage of soil and pots with louvered shutters or plywood panels. Or install curtain rods along the top of the bench and hang plastic or bamboo curtains that can be pushed aside for access to your supplies. You might build cabinets instead of benches and top these with waterproof trays filled with pebbles to accommodate pots of your favorite plants and bulbs. Cover the floor in this area with slate or vinyl; furnish with a comfortable chair or two, or perhaps a small table and chairs to make a flowery dining area. Fluorescent lights or decorative hanging lamps will make your plant room as delightful by night as by day.

A large free-standing greenhouse can be a delightful garden or game room that can be decorated like any other room except that consideration must always be given to the effects of humidity and condensation that are inevitable in a large glassed-in area. Select draperies and furniture coverings that are moistureproof or can be made so. Probably you won't want wallpaper anywhere, but even that can be made

26. A combination of lean-to and even-span greenhouses converts a cantilevered balcony to a usable, enjoyable living-growing area.

highly moisture-resistant, as can painted surfaces. Cover the floor with vinyl patterned with big black and white squares—most practical and attractive.

A new indoor-outdoor carpeting made of a synthetic fiber is ideal for a greenhouse used partly for gardening and partly for living. This remarkable new carpeting is impervious to all seasons and all weather, heavy traffic, rot, mildew; it does not shrink, stretch, fade or discolor, can be washed down with a hose, and is available in several colors.

8

How to Make
Your Hobby Pay

Of the several thousands who join the ranks of hobby greenhouse gardeners each year, few, I am sure, do so with the intention of making money from their hobby. Yet it is surprising how many gardeners under glass eventually use their talents in this direction.

My first ventures in greenhouse gardening were for the sheer joy of nurturing seedlings to maturity and possessing beauty of form and color available, to my way of thinking, in no other way. Yet it wasn't long before a chance remark of mine opened up the possibility that my greenhouse activities might produce a fair return on my investment of time and money.

A greenhouse bursting with cymbidium and cattleya orchid blossoms one early spring caused me to remark that I had so many flowers I didn't know what to do with them. A friend who heard my comment spoke to a florist—who offered to buy all the cut orchids I cared to sell; it was as simple as that! Each spring my greenhouse brims with blossoms and I think that perhaps I should accept the florist's offer. But I keep putting it off—I just can't seem to part with any of the flowers, at least not in that way. I'd rather give them to friends.

The market is there
The point is: there is a ready market for the plant products of anyone who might like to turn his hobby into an income-producing pasttime, and not only for orchids. Home-greenhouse gardeners often find

a market for foliage plants, or for seedlings for outdoor gardens in spring; some specialize in one kind of plant, as African-violets, geraniums, even herbs; others find corsages profitable.

Research the possibilities

If suddenly you find yourself with excess plant material and think you might like to sell it to provide a little extra income, or if you are contemplating your retirement from business and feel you would like to fill your days with profitable activity, consider all the aspects carefully, and approach the project slowly.

It is one thing to find that you are growing more than you can possibly use for your own pleasure and enjoyment; it is an entirely different thing to be faced with the necessity of delivering on a promise to produce 100 geranium cuttings, 100 pots of begonias, or dozens or hundreds of annual seedlings for a market that is governed by the calendar. You may feel sure now that it is just as easy to grow dozens or hundreds as it is to grow a few and that to meet the challenge will be sufficiently rewarding to make the extra effort worth your while. But there is a very real possibility that when you *have* to produce, your joyous hobby will become an overwhelming burden.

If you really feel that you would like to try your hand at selling, consider carefully what plants you can grow easily, quickly, and inexpensively. Decide upon the most appealing way to offer your material to your potential market. Consult the local office of the Better Business Bureau regarding pricing for a profit. If they cannot help you with this phase of the marketing, perhaps they will be able to suggest someone who can.

Talk to your local florist—no one is more alert to market trends than he, and his advice will be sound and sensible.

Selling wholesale

You may learn, as other hobby gardeners have learned, that the florist you consult for advice may himself need certain plant material that you can contract to supply, and perhaps that will be all the work you will care to handle.

When you have decided upon your product and your price, talk to the manager of your local supermarket or variety store; show him your product, attractively packaged and reasonably priced. If you find a market here, do not promise more than you can comfortably deliver, but work out an arrangement whereby you can start slowly and build gradually. Most stores of this type seem to prefer foliage plants, which would be the ideal kinds for your first selling efforts since they are not limited to one season of the year but can be produced and sold the year around. It would be unwise, at the beginning, to attempt to sell highly seasonal plants for which there is a demand for only a short period each year. That would leave you with a long period of time with little or no return on your investment.

Selling retail from your greenhouse

You may find it more interesting to sell directly from your greenhouse to customers who come to you. In this case, you will not have to confine yourself to one or two types of plants, but can offer a wide selection unless, of course, you decide to build a reputation as a specialist. You will not be under the pressure of delivery dates since your entire stock, whatever it may be at any given time, will be available to any and all customers. This type of operation sometimes proves to be the most satisfactory, as it allows an opportunity for income without the pressures connected with a commercial endeavor.

If you live in a rural community, you may find a ready market for annual and perennial seedlings, tomato and various other vegetable plants for spring gardens.

Those who specialize in carnations, camellias, or orchids might find corsages to be profitable, especially around prom and graduation time. Corsage preparation is simple and inexpensive: some florist's tape, fine wire, tiny plastic tubes equipped with sponges, and a few simple twists of the wrist and you will have attractive items to sell. With a little practice, you will soon turn out professional-looking corsages, and word-of-mouth advertising will bring you all the business you can handle.

Some gardeners eliminate the tediousness and tying-up of space required to sow seeds and transplant seedlings by purchasing established plant material in flats or in 2-inch pots and growing it on to saleable size. Mature stock can then be marketed locally or by mail and your business activity may be more easily controlled.

Selling by mail

Certain types of plant materials lend themselves to mail-order selling. If your interest lies in this direction, check with your local postmaster for regulations governing use of the mails for interstate shipments of live plant material. The demand for plants sold by mail may be greater than a local neighborhood operation might create, and you must be in a position to supply the demand, or you not only will not turn a profit but most likely will lose your investment. You must have the materials, equipment, and abilities to pack plants for safe shipment; you must know whether it is too hot or too cold to ship, not only where you are but where your customer is; and you may find yourself burdened intolerably with correspondence.

Stay on the right side of the law

If you contemplate a business venture, the very first thing you should do is check with your local regulatory boards about zoning laws and regulations. If you sell only a few surplus plants to friends, and no trucks or advertising signs are evident around your property, few objections will be heard from neighbors *but* you may be violating local zoning, fire, or building codes.

In many instances, residential-district zoning regulations restrict sales to only what is grown on the premises; no other material or supplies may be offered, even though they have a direct relationship to your major item. Some areas forbid all local selling, and business must be restricted to wholesale only, or to selling by mail. And even though you may be operating strictly within the law when you start, changes in local zoning regulations may inaugurate harsher restrictions that would limit or prohibit expansion or put you out of business altogether. Discuss your plans with fire and building inspectors, check zoning regulations, and avoid the possibility of disappointment or frustration *after* your venture is under way.

As you can see, there are many possibilities for turning your hobby gardening activities into a profitable pasttime. If you contemplate a business venture, investigate all the aspects of the undertaking. When you finally decide to have your business cards printed, may your endeavors be successful and rewarding!

Part Two

Grow!

9

Fun Your First Year

The point of greenhouse gardening is to have fun. Don't load your-self with more plants and projects than you can enjoy—at least, try not to! I know well the hazards of greenhouse enthusiasms but I, too, try to limit my desire for an increasing variety of plants as well as a cer-tain amount of yearly experimentation. Also, don't let yourself be over-whelmed by the instructions in this book or in any other book or manual. Don't ignore altogether the "musts" and the "must-nots," but you don't have to be a slave to rules. Plants are tolerant of considerable variations in culture, provided you do not let them cook under the glass or get too parched for water.

In any case, there are no hard-and-fast rules for success. You will find that your plants grow best when you develop an affinity for them, and this comes from close observation of the plants plus a large applica-tion of common sense. Just take one step at a time. Master the funda-mentals before you succumb to the excitement of special techniques or the challenge of difficult subjects.

First-year schedule

If you decide to grow bench plants (planting directly in soil con-tained in benches, in much the same way as you grow plants in your outdoor garden) select only two or three kinds for your first year. By the time you have planted seeds, potted bulbs, transplanted seedlings or rooted-cuttings into pots, and developed a good watering and fer-tilizing program, your greenhouse is likely to take up most of your free time. You will find that watering on sunny days is a different busi-

97

27. Frame supports for snapdragons fasten directly to bench; glass shelves provide extra growing space without casting shadows or cutting off light from plants below.

ness from watering in cloudy or rainy weather, and that ventilating can be time consuming until you work out a fairly definite schedule for it. Soil preparation can become a major project if you let it, but I hope you won't; and only experience will indicate when to fertilize and what amount to give. So try to restrict your first fine enthusiasm just a little. Let me say again: enjoy what you are doing, and *let* your greenhouse give you the pleasure and relaxation you anticipated.

Unless you have decided definitely on the plants you want to grow, I recommend a cool greenhouse of 45 to 50 F (that is *night temperature*, you know) for your first venture with snapdragons, stocks, geraniums, and a few hardy bulbs—perhaps tulips, hyacinths and daffodils. Plants grown cool are less susceptible to the insects and diseases that develop in a warm, moist atmosphere. Snapdragons and stocks can be grown in flats, but I suggest that you fill one whole bench with soil just for these two. Together they will provide a riot of color, marvelous fragrance, and an abundance of flowers to cut. Grow the ever-favorite geranium in pots. Perhaps you can lift some big plants from your outside garden or window box. Or your local florist may have some in the fall, and house-plant mail-order houses can supply some lovely unusual kinds. Force, say, six pans of bulbs; they will make your first spring excitingly beautiful. All the know-how for handling them is given in Chapter 11.

With this seemingly limited objective of two kinds of bench plants, one decorative kind of pot plant, and a few pans of hardy bulbs, you will still be trying your hand at many greenhouse techniques. When the seeds of stocks and snapdragons germinate and the seedlings form their first true leaves (usually when they reach 1 to 1½ inches in height) you will be transplanting them directly into a bench; as the potted geraniums put out new shoots you can increase your supply by taking cuttings. By the time the bench plants are well established, you can bring into the greenhouse (from their cold place outdoors) the potted bulbs for forcing. Even with all these plants, there will be occasions this first year when blooms will be scarce, but you will be so busy with your various projects that you will scarcely miss them.

However, once your snapdragons and stocks begin to bloom, you will have a seemingly endless supply of flowers. Keep cutting them, and the striking display will continue. Perhaps you will still yearn for other favorites. But keep it simple the first year while you are learning, and your future greenhouse gardening will be more richly rewarding, for you will have given yourself time to learn by doing, to get the "feel" of growing under glass, and you will be the happier for it.

Second-year schedule

Then, during your first summer, you can work up a more ambitious schedule for your second season with the purpose of having color in your greenhouse throughout the year. Here are suggestions for twelve months of color in a cool greenhouse (45 to 50 F night temperature):

January	stocks (*Mathiola incana*)	sow seed late July to early August
February	snapdragons (*Antirrhinum majus*)	sow seed in October
March	poor-man's-orchid (*Schizanthus*)	sow seed in August
April	tulips, daffodils, hyacinths	pot bulbs in October

28. Well-prepared seed flats and pots furnish hundreds of healthy seedlings. (ROCHE PHOTO)

May	sweet-peas (*Lathyrus odoratus*)	sow seed in November
June	pot-marigold (*Calendula officinalis*)	sow seed in November
July	gloxinias (*Sinningia speciosa*)	pot tubers in February; place in warmest part of greenhouse
August	geraniums (*Pelargonium*)	take cuttings early June
September	*Tulbaghia cepacea*	pot rhizomes in August
October	chrysanthemums	take cuttings of late types in May
November	bouvardia	buy plants in May to mature in greenhouse
December	cineraria (*Senecio cruentus*)	sow seed in May

You can improvise

The major expense of greenhouse construction comes the first year, so you may want to postpone other purchases to hold your operating costs to a minimum. Improvise wherever and whenever you can. Suggestions to help you do this are given at the end of Chapter 4. Keep in mind that you can rig bench frames for your snapdragons, and dig topsoil from your garden and pasteurize it in your oven to save the expense of buying soil. You can settle for a dirt floor the first year—it is not so attractive as brick, slate, or wood slats and it might be slippery and muddy occasionally, but it is practical and economical.

Sharp kitchen knives and large mixing spoons are substitutes for strong greenhouse scissors and trowels; with careful regulation of water flow, plants can be watered successfully with a garden hose; and you will be surprised how many flower pots from discarded gift plants your friends will be delighted to unload on you. Scrubbed with a Lysol solution and a wire brush, they will be as good as new. Then there are the possibilities of milk cartons—quart and half-gallon containers, well scoured and with one side removed, make excellent waterproof seed flats.

So use your imagination and your ingenuity—it's half the fun of your first year of gardening under glass.

The easiest plants for winter flowers

Flowers in winter are one of the great joys of a garden under glass. When nature goes to sleep outdoors and the greenhouse wakes to vivid life, our every effort is rewarded. Among the plants that bloom—and I value a number of others just for foliage—are many of very easy culture. Here are some of my favorites that thrive in a cool greenhouse (about 45 to 50 F at night) and do well for me at 52 F, which seems to be the constant night temperature in my greenhouse. Slight variations seem to have little effect on these amenable plants, but even so, I try to place them in areas where there is little fluctuation from the 52 F setting.

Many other plants can be grown under the same conditions, as the list (Plants for cool greenhouses) in Part IV shows, but I suggest the following to you because they mature and bloom fairly quickly. (Others that I enjoy take longer, and you might find the waiting tedious, especially your first year when you are eager to fill your greenhouse with color and fragrance.) You will find the cultural instructions for each of the following plants in the alphabetical list of plants in Part III of this book.

>Blue lace-flower (*Trachymene caerulea*)
>California-poppy (*Eschscholzia californica*)
>Carnation (*Dianthus Caryophyllus*)
>Floss-flower (*Ageratum Houstonianum*)

Forget-me-not (*Myosotis sylvatica*)
Lobelia (*Lobelia Erinus*)
Nasturtium (*Tropaeolum majus*)
Nemesia strumosa
Pot-marigold (*Calendula officinalis*)
Snapdragon (*Antirrhinum majus*)
Stock (*Mathiola incana*)
Sweet-alyssum (*Lobularia maritima*)
Sweet-pea (*Lathyrus odoratus*)

10

Benched, Potted, and Hanging Plants

The plants in your greenhouse will probably be grown in one or more of these: benches, pots, or suspended containers such as baskets. There are a few exceptions—you may want to fasten an epiphytic plant to a piece of treefern or bark, and perhaps you will put some climbing plants, shrubs, or plant collections directly in ground beds in the greenhouse. But until you are experienced and have become acquainted with the variations of climate in corners and different levels and areas of your greenhouse, you will most likely use some of each of benches, pots, and baskets.

BENCH PLANTS

When you want an abundant, continuous supply of flowers to cut, grow the plants directly in benches filled with soil, in much the same manner as you operate a cutting garden out-of-doors. If you want flowers for cutting throughout the year, you will have to plan and time things so that when one kind has finished flowering, it can be replaced at once with another.

The plants most commonly grown in benches are:

> Carnation (*Dianthus Caryophyllus*)
> Chryanthemum
> Snapdragon (*Antirrhinum majus*)
> Stock (*Mathiola incana*)
> Sweet-pea (*Lathyrus odoratus*)

Others that can be grown in benches by the gardener who wants lots
of them available for cutting are:

> Baby's-breath (*Gypsophila elegans*)
> Bachelor-button (*Centaurea cyanus*)
> Blue-lace-flower (*Trachymene caerulea*)
> Candytuft (*Iberis*)
> China aster (*Callistephus chinensis*)
> *Clarkia elegans*
> Feverfew (*Chrysanthemum Parthenium*)
> Forget-me-not (*Myosotis sylvatica*)
> Larkspur (*Delphinium*)
> Marigold (*Tagetes*)
> Mignonette (*Reseda odorata*)
> *Nemesia strumosa*
> Pansy (*Viola tricolor*)
> Pot-marigold (*Calendula officinalis*)
> Salpiglossis
> Transvaal-daisy (*Gerberia Jamesonii*)
> Violet (*Viola odorata*)

POT PLANTS

The universally used kind of container for plants is a pot—made of
clay, plastic, wood, ceramic, or some other rigid material. Shapes,
colors, sizes, and drainage arrangements of such containers are endless
in their variations. The important and useful thing about pots is that
they provide individual housing for each plant, and each plant can be
moved and cared for according to its needs and the gardener's facilities.

There is hardly a flowering or green- or variegated-foliage plant that
will not grow in a pot. Individual plants of the kinds recommended for
bench growing do just as well in a pot when you want, for example,
only a few snapdragons and not arms full. Plants that like to trail, hang,
or sprawl will do so in a pot that is suspended. All things considered,
pots are the most useful items in your greenhouse, and you will probably acquire a formidable array of kinds, sizes, and shapes.

How to pot a plant

In time, seedlings and cuttings outgrow their first small containers
and must be transferred to larger quarters. Indeed, this repotting goes

29. HOW TO REPOT A PLANT. Tap inverted pot gently against bench while supporting contents, scrape away old soil and dead roots, center soil-ball in larger pot (if needed), fill in and around with fresh soil, and firm gently with thumbs.

on all the time with both young plants and those long established in the greenhouse.

Let a plant stay in a pot until the pot is crowded with roots. Here's how to check on root growth: water the plant well; hold it in your right hand, place your left hand over the soil with the plant held between your first and second fingers. Invert the pot. Tap the rim smartly against the edge of a bench. The plant will drop out easily into your hand.

If the rootball has taken the shape of the pot and covered the soil with roots, shift the plant to a somewhat larger pot. If it is in a 2½-inch pot, shift to one no larger than a 4; if it is in a 3, shift to a 5. Don't move plants on too fast, for a too-large pot is just as bad as one too small.

Prepare the new pot with drainage material—one or more pieces of broken clay pot over the hole—and then a layer of gravel or coarse soil. Pour in potting soil above this but not too much, since space must be left for the rootball. Water the plant to be repotted. When moisture has penetrated sufficiently to let you remove the pot, have a look at the rootball. If you are repotting older plants that have been growing a year or more in the same pot, get rid of as much old soil as you can.

30. *Chaenostoma fastigiatum* produces racemes of tiny starlike white flowers continuously. (MERRY GARDENS PHOTO)

31. *Citrus mitis,* the calamondin orange, has fragrant flowers, green fruit, and tiny ripe oranges all at the same time and practically the year around. (MERRY GARDENS PHOTO)

32. *Exacum affine* stays small, covers itself with small fragrant lavender flowers. (MERRY GARDENS PHOTO)

With a dibble or other pointed object carefully scrape off soil and dead roots. Then hold the plant in place in the partially filled new pot, and add more soil. Firm this around the rootball with your fingers or a stick. As you work, occasionally strike the bottom of the pot against a bench to settle the soil and fill in any air pockets.

Finally, water the repotted plant lightly from above, or sub-irrigate by standing it in a vessel of water until the top soil feels moist. Shade the plant for a few days to offset the possible shock of transplanting. Then return to sunshine—unless the plant is a shade-loving type—and resume your feeding schedule.

In the course of time, most plants need this repotting to larger quarters. Some won't, however, because they thrive and bloom better when the "shoe fits tight." But they all need nourishment, and you can provide this without repotting: simply replace the upper inch or so of old soil with a fresh rich mixture and augment this with applications of liquid fertilizer about every two weeks in periods of the plant's active growth.

Some of the easiest flowering plants to grow in pots are abutilon (flowering-maple), acacia, *Ardisia crispa* (coral-berry), azaleas, *Belo-*

33. *Jacobinia carnea*, a marvelous large, bushy pot plant with beautiful pink flower plumes. (MERRY GARDENS PHOTO)

perone guttata (shrimp-plant), bouvardia, calceolaria, *Carissa grandiflora* (Natal-plum), crossandra, cyclamen, *Euphorbia pulcherrima* (poinsettia), *Euphorbia splendens* (crown-of-thorns), *Felicia amelloides* (blue-marguerite), gardenia, heliotrope, impatiens, *Osmanthus fragrans* (sweet-olive), primrose, roses, schizanthus (poor-man's-orchid), *Senecio cruentus* (cineraria), and zygocactus (Christmas cactus).

And here are a few easy-to-grow foliage plants for pots: *Aucuba japonica variegata* (gold-dust-plant), caladium, *Codiaeum variegatum* (croton), coleus, *Gynura aurantiaca* (velvet-plant), peperomia, pilea, and pittosporum.

BASKET AND SHELF PLANTS
TRAILERS, CLIMBERS, AND VINES

You may visualize your garden under glass as a profusion of bloom and a riot of color, but you will certainly be missing something if you do not include some of the interesting and decorative trailing, climbing, and vining plants. Their distinctive leaf patterns, unusual forms and growth habits, and (on some) magnificent flowers, provide the frame that completes the picture made by your winter garden. They add grace and decoration to the interior of your greenhouse.

Many lovely plants whose nature it is to trail or hang, or even sprawl, are cultivated and displayed to advantage only when they are grown in a container that is suspended, as a basket or pot that hangs from above, or a pot placed on a high shelf.

To some plants nature has given the irrepressible urge and need to climb, clamber, or twine and twist. These plants can be grown in pots or other stable containers placed so the plants will grow up the inside of the glass, thereby shading tender plants on benches; or they can climb on a trellis, wire-mesh, or lattice arrangement of twine, against the solid wall of a lean-to greenhouse or even as floral "walls" to divide sections of benches.

Containers for hanging plants

Catalogues available from nurserymen list a variety of types and styles of containers for trailing plants: open-work wire baskets, metal baskets, plastic lattice-type baskets, pots with attached saucers, even ceramic containers or baskets of Mexican fernwood or redwood. I prefer the open-work wire basket for my own plantings; they seem to be more decorative when lined with sphagnum moss and the bits and

34. Shelves and hanging pots relieve overflowing benches. (GENEREUX PHOTO)

35. Begonia 'Shippy's Garland', beautiful in a suspended container or on a shelf. (MERRY GARDENS PHOTO)

pieces of moss wander through the openings. No matter what container you select, basic preparation is the same, and quite simple.

How to plant a basket

Line the basket with moss (either coarse sphagnum or sheetmoss) that has been soaked thoroughly and pressed firmly to remove excess water. This lining holds the soil mixture in the basket and helps retain moisture in the soil. Next, fill the basket to within about 1 inch of the top with a soil mixture consisting of equal parts of clean sharp sand, well-rotted manure, and garden loam, leafmold, or peatmoss. Water well and let drain before planting.

Care must be taken in the selection of the material to be planted in a basket. Plants mature rapidly under the ideal controlled conditions of ventilation, heat, and humidity provided under glass, and what seems to be a sparse planting when baskets are being prepared will, in short order, fill them to overflowing. In small baskets, plant no more than three evenly spaced plants to a basket. In large baskets, four or five plants can be accommodated depending upon your choice of plant material. Think of the basket as a square—place one plant in each corner and one in the center.

Water thoroughly, using a fine spray to help prevent loss of moisture in the leaves due to transplanting, and to settle the plant into the soil mixture. Do not allow soil and moss to dry out or growth will be checked, and baskets will be a disappointment. It will be difficult for you to know the moisture condition of the soil, as the plants will be above eye level, so apply water liberally. Moss provides adequate drainage to prevent water-logging of soil. Liberal watering, however, leaches nutrients from the soil, so a regular feeding program with liquid fertilizer every two weeks is necessary.

For an interesting variety of foliage, color of bloom, and growth characteristics, try various combinations of the trailing and climbing plants listed below. Most of these are for a cool house with a temperature range of 45 to 50 F, but you will find that warmer temperatures near the roof of the greenhouse make it possible to include a few requiring a more moderate climate.

Some of the best are: begonias (tuberous hanging kinds), bougainvillea, browallia, *Campanula isophylla,* ceropegia, chlorophytum, clerodendrum, episcia, fuchsia, *Hedera Helix* (English ivy), hoya (waxplant), lantana, manettia (firecracker-vine), oxalis, passiflora (passionflower), pelargonium (ivy-leaved geranium), *Plumbago capensis* (leadwort), *Saxifraga sarmentosa* (strawberry-begonia), streptosolen (orange-browallia), *Trachelospermum jasminoides* (star-jasmine), and tradescantia (inch-plant).

36. *Jasminum gracile magnificum,* graceful basket plant. (MERRY GARDENS PHOTO)

37. HOW TO PREPARE A HANGING BASKET. Line basket with coarse sphagnum moss or sheetmoss, fill in with planting medium, insert plants at evenly spaced intervals, and enjoy the beauty of ivy-leaved geraniums, lantanas, pendent tuberous begonias, and other favorite trailing plants.

11

Fascinating Hardy and Tender Bulbs

Bulbs are classified as *hardy* and *tender*. Hardy bulbs must be given a period of cold darkness during which they develop strong root systems before growth of foliage is permitted. Tender bulbs cannot survive such a cold or freezing temperature. Technically, not all of the plants discussed in this chapter have true bulbs—some grow from corms, rhizomes, tubers, fleshy roots, or other kind of underground stem—but as all are handled in much the same way, they are included.

Hardy and tender bulbs in wide variety are easy to grow, and they fit nicely into a greenhouse program. If you start operating your greenhouse in September and get your seed sowing done then, bulbs can be potted and stored in October, and out of the way before it is time to transplant seedlings—you will be able to devote yourself to one major task at a time.

HARDY BULBS

There is nothing quite so delightful or rewarding in the dead of winter than to step into a greenhouse filled with golden daffodils, brilliant tulips of many colors, and fragrant white or blue hyacinths. Literally, you find yourself in springtime, not merely for a day or two, but continuously, for weeks on end—all this with a few days' effort! (See Color Plate VIII.)

Most of the hardy bulbs are the spring-flowering kinds, and they are true bulbs, that is, they are composed of fleshy scales that protect

113

38. Hardy bulbs potted in October can be forced to bloom under glass while snow covers the outdoor garden. (ROCHE PHOTO)

a bud at the base, the embryo flower forms inside the bulb, and the bulbs are usually encased in a very thin, dry skin.

"Forcing" these bulbs means only that you beguile them into blooming in your greenhouse weeks or months earlier than they would bloom naturally out-of-doors. They must be potted, placed in a cold, dark location while roots develop, then brought into a cool greenhouse where foliage and flowers will mature.

Hardy bulbs may be potted any time from early October to the middle of December. Six to eight weeks must be allowed for root development, so plan to do your potting as early as possible, or according to the flowering schedule you desire.

Buy quality bulbs

Good bulbs are not inexpensive, but it is better to buy fewer good bulbs, if necessary, than to settle for a larger quantity of average-quality bulbs. Send for catalogues (usually they are profusely illustrated in color) from several bulb specialists. You will find many colors and types of tulips, hyacinths, and daffodils to choose from, but you will be better satisfied if you select bulbs described as good forcing varieties. Select carefully, and you will have a brilliant display for several weeks in spring, before your other plants are in flower. Do not overlook the white-flowered plants—nothing is more pleasing than a burst of white against a background of color.

Bulb dealers fill orders for top-quality bulbs in the sequence in which they are received, so assure yourself of getting what you want by placing your order early.

Precooled bulbs

Most bulb dealers offer a few *pre-cooled* forcing varieties for very early greenhouse flowering. If you cannot obtain pre-cooled kinds, you can condition them yourself by placing the unpotted bulbs in an unheated garage or other building for several weeks. My first bulbs, acquired late in the season because my greenhouse was not in operation until January, were purchased in the local variety store and kept in the refrigerator for three weeks. Pre-cooled bulbs must be potted immediately upon receipt or upon being removed from their cool treatment, and of course they require the same cold rooting period that all hardy bulbs must have, as described later in this chapter.

Soil mixture for hardy bulbs

A soil mixture consisting of two parts garden loam, one part clean sharp sand, and one part peatmoss is fine. Little if any fertilizer is needed, since high-quality bulbs store their own supply of food. If you think your soil might be inadequate in nutrients, add bonemeal to your mixture—it acts very slowly and provides nourishment without damaging roots.

Bulb-pans

Special pots called *bulb-pans*—actually shallow flower pots that are wider than they are deep—are best for potting tulips, hyacinths, and daffodils; 4-inch-deep flats are also adequate. For the most attractive display, plant three or four bulbs of one kind to a bulb-pan, depending on the size of bulbs and pan. If flats are used, bulbs can be spaced about 1 inch apart. A single bulb may be planted in a small pot, but the flowering display will not be very dramatic.

Potting

Place a layer of pot shards or gravel in the bottom of the pot, then a layer of charcoal to "sweeten" the soil, then a layer of soil mixture. At this point, you will have to predetermine the depth to which the bulbs will be set into the pot in order to leave about 1 inch of space above the top of the soil when potting has been completed. When you have the proper depth of soil, place the bulbs in position gently on this soil bed and fill in around them and over the tips with soil. Shake the pot to settle the soil around the bulbs. Water thoroughly; this one watering will be sufficient until growth begins. Label or mark the pots in some manner so they can be easily identified when you start to bring them into the greenhouse for forcing.

Rooting period

For the root-making period, the bulbs may be handled in any of several ways. Select the method most practical for you:

Trench. Dig a trench about a foot deep in a well-drained section of the garden. Cover the bottom with 3 to 4 inches of sand, cinders, or gravel to assure good drainage. Place the bulb-pans or flats on this base and cover with soil. Just before freezing temperatures are expected, cover the trench with a layer of straw, salt-hay, or leaves. This

39. HARDY BULBS. Original plantings and subsequent bulb divisions receive the same treatment: use a sharp knife to divide or separate offsets, pot, and place in cold, dark location for root development. Inverted pots protect new top growth from damage or deformity.

keeps the ground from freezing solid and enables you to remove the pots with ease, once the roots have developed.

Coldframe. If you have a coldframe, place the pots or flats in it and cover with salt-hay, leaves, or sand. Put on top sash when temperature goes to freezing.

Above ground. Along one side of your greenhouse outside, place a row of stakes about a foot out from the wall. Enclose the staked area with a temporary, makeshift retaining wall of screen or boards. Place a layer of sand on the ground in the enclosed area, and position the pots or flats on this sand base. Fill in, around, and over the pots to a depth of about a foot with leaves. This worked very well for me one winter.

Refrigerator. Fill a refrigerator (the old one in the garage or basement that you use for soft drinks during summer) with potted bulb-pans and set the temperature control at its lowest point. Open the door as seldom as possible, though you will have to check the pots about once a week for signs that the soil might be drying (because of efficient air circulation in a refrigerator); most likely you will need to water the pots several times during the eight-week rooting period.

Even though this is a period for *root* development, some plants will start top growth before they are ready to be removed to the greenhouse. Therefore, do not place one pot directly on top of another. In any of the four cold areas suggested above, however, you can make double tiers by inverting an empty pot over each one in the bottom layer and then stacking a second layer on top of the inverted pots.

Bringing rooted bulbs into the greenhouse

Occasionally, a hardy bulb will develop sufficient roots in about six weeks to be ready for forcing, but usually eight full weeks should be allowed. By the end of the eight-week period, the pot should contain a mass of well-developed roots which have started to grow through the drainage hole in the bottom of the pot. That, in fact, is how you will know that a pot is ready to go to the greenhouse—when you see roots growing through the drainage hole.

When this stage has been reached, you may start bringing the pots into the greenhouse for forcing into bloom. Bulbs are not injured by a longer cold storage, however, so you will not find it necessary to transfer all pots to the greenhouse at the same time. If you have marked the pots carefully, you will be able to select one or two of each kind for an interesting display. A succession of bloom is possible over a long period of time if you bring in only a few pots at a time.

It is important, when the bulbs come into the greenhouse, to raise their temperature gradually to assure development of foliage and stems before forcing the blooms. Water well and place the pots in a cool, dark place, as under a bench, for about 10 to 14 days. A 50 F temperature is ideal for this period of development. If stems do not seem to be stretching properly, place a section of cardboard tube (such as the core of a roll of waxed paper or aluminum foil) or a homemade paper cone over the top growth. Stems will "reach" for the small area of light at the top of the tube or cone. Inspect periodically, and when stem is of adequate length, remove the tube so as not to interfere with or deform the flower.

At the end of this two-week period, move the pots onto the bench in full sunlight, since more warmth is necessary to promote flowering. Water freely until flowers open. Then move the plants out of direct sun so flowers will last longer.

If you maintain a temperature of 50 F, it will take about five weeks to force bulbs into bloom; if the temperature is raised to 60 F, blooms will appear in three to four weeks. But heed a word of caution: don't be carried away with the idea of raising the temperature simply to force bulbs—there may be other plant material in your greenhouse that will not tolerate a 10-degree increase in temperature. Also, bulbs that are grown slowly and cool will reward you with stronger, healthier, longer-lasting blossoms.

Care after flowering

Once a hardy bulb has been forced, it cannot be forced satisfactorily a second year. It should be discarded or transferred to the outdoor garden. If you plan to use it outdoors, continue to water and give plenty of sun until the foliage ripens, to guarantee the development of the new flower bud and stem within the bulb. Remove bulbs from pots and plant in their permanent outdoor location, any time after the ground is workable. They will not flower their first year outdoors, probably, but after that they should perform very satisfactorily.

The small hardy bulbs

The small hardy bulbs that we are so happy to see flowering out-doors in spring respond to greenhouse forcing as easily as the more spectacular tulips, hyacinths, and daffodils. You may not have time or space to devote to these small, modest flowers the first year in your greenhouse, but try to work in a few pots of crocus, grape-hyacinths (*Muscari*), scillas, and snowdrops (*Galanthus*) anyway.

TENDER BULBS

Tender and half-hardy bulbs, though sometimes grown in cool temperatures, cannot stand the freezing or very cold temperatures needed by hardy bulbs. Tender "bulbs" include not only true bulbs, but plants that grow from other types of underground stems, as rhizomes, corms, tubers, and fleshy roots. In many instances, tender bulbs can be potted and grown at times of the year other than their natural season, provided, of course, you can obtain the bulbs at off-times of the year and can provide their needed conditions.

Tender bulbs have two appealing characteristics: the many different kinds of flowers, from the tremendous lily-like blossoms of amaryllis to the delicate, deliciously fragrant freesia; and the fact that they can be potted and started immediately into growth. Some, as the paperwhite narcissus and the dainty French-Roman hyacinths, grow and produce flowers quite rapidly.

Soil, potting, and culture

Most tender and half-hardy bulbs should be potted in a mixture of two parts garden loam, one part peatmoss, and one part sand, with a little bonemeal added to promote continuous growth. Screening the soil mixture through a half-inch mesh is beneficial, as the roots must be able to move through the soil without obstructions.

Potting procedure is the same as described earlier for hardy bulbs. Place some drainage material in the bottom of the pot, add soil mixture, plant the bulbs, and water thoroughly. Keep the pots under the bench for a week or two, then move them to the bench to good light.

Proper watering is important. After the initial thorough watering, water sparingly until top growth is well started; then increase the supply of water to insure continuous development of the foliage and flowers.

Grow some without soil

Another nice thing about some of these tender bulbs is that they do not have to be grown in soil, but can be set in containers of pebbles filled with water. The pebbles support the bulb, which should be placed so that half the bulb extends above the pebbles; if the container is kept filled with water to the top of the pebbles, sufficient moisture will be available for substantial root growth. Add a piece or two of charcoal to the pebbles to keep the water "sweet."

Paperwhite narcissus and French-Roman hyacinths, especially, can be grown in this manner. A few containers planted in this fashion placed on the shelves in your greenhouse lend a daintiness and fragrance that is most appealing; or you can move them into your home as soon as they have been forced into bloom.

Care after flowering

Tender bulbs vary considerably in their growth habits—some remain evergreen, some even flower almost all year, and some require definite dormant periods. The care for each is given in Part III.

Many kinds to select from

I suggest that you try only one or two kinds of tender bulbs from the following list your first season (in addition to your hardy bulbs)—not that they are difficult to grow, but to allow for a different selection the following season to add interest and variety to your gardening program.

>Achimenes (magic-flower)
>Agapanthus (lily-of-the-Nile)
>Alstroemeria (Peruvian-lily)
>Anemone
>Begonia, tuberous
>Clivia (Kafir-lily)
>Crinum
>Dahlia
>Eucharis (Amazon-lily)
>Freesia
>Gladiolus
>Gloriosa (glory-lily)
>Haemanthus (blood-lily)

Hippeastrum (amaryllis)
Hymenocallis (Peruvian-daffodil)
Iris
Lachenalia (cape-cowslip)
Lilium (lily)
Nerine (Guernsey-lily)
Ornithogalum (star-of-Bethlehem; chincherinchee)
Polianthes (tuberose)
Ranunculus
Sinningia (gloxinia)
Tritonia
Tulbaghia
Vallota (Scarborough-lily)
Veltheimia
Zantedeschia (calla-lily)

12

Hobby Plants for Special Pleasure

The complaint of greenhouse gardeners—and it is universal—is that our world is too full of a number of plants. We think that we are not looking for specialties but rather how, in the interest of sanity, to avoid them! Yet, many of us find ourselves attracted to certain plants to the point of excluding all others; and when we join a plant society devoted to a favorite plant, the pleasure in our accomplishments knows no bounds.

As you experience the joys of gardening under glass, you may find that certain plants appeal irresistibly to *you*. You may be able to limit yourself to a half-dozen favorites, either because you admire them so much or because your gardening time is limited to a few weekend hours, and growing a compatible group gives you a lot of flowers with some time left to appreciate them.

Perhaps in time you will get more fun from a greenhouse devoted to one plant, as African-violets; or to one family of plants, as orchids or gesneriads; or to one class of plants, as cacti and succulents. Then in a few years you may turn with enthusiasm to quite different ones.

Begonias are unbelievably easy to grow, and you could soon fill a greenhouse with nothing but begonias because there are so many kinds of them, with great diversity of form, color, season, and culture. A greenhouse devoted to, or with a good-sized section for, cacti and other succulent plants can be a mighty interesting place, for what group includes such peculiar forms, such startling flowers?

123

Camellias are among the most exquisite of shrubs for greenhouse gardening, and while one or two tubs of them may content you for a while, you *could* give over almost your whole greenhouse to them, particularly if it is a glass-to-ground type. Geraniums could claim your undivided attention the year around: fancy and scented leaves, flowering giants and amusing miniatures, trailing ivy-leaved kinds for baskets, and elegant regal or Lady Washingtons. Perhaps you will fall in love with ballerina-like fuchsias, and want baskets and standards and pots of them all through your greenhouse.

Maybe you will start with African-violets, and become enthralled by the other members of the gesneriad family with its tremendous variations of flower and form, from big exuberant trailing columneas to what may be the tiniest plant in cultivation, *Sinningia pusilla*.

40. *Begonia manicata aureo-maculata.* The many and varied forms and colors of begonias have led hobby greenhouse gardeners to specialize in them. (MERRY GARDENS PHOTO)

41. *Nephrolepis exaltata* 'Fluffy Ruffles'. Consider the filmy and feathery, or solid and leathery, fronds or leaves of intriguing ferns if your greenhouse is warm and humid. (MERRY GARDENS PHOTO)

Bromeliads—there are enough to keep a fancier happy for the rest of his gardening life; and the same can be said for ferns. Or maybe you are one who will find satisfaction in growing as many kinds of variegated foliage plants as you can, especially if you have a north-facing greenhouse.

Are you a good cook as well as a gardener? Then how about herbs? Maybe you will start with part of a bench of these, just to have them available for a gourmet touch, but can you stop there? Probably not, especially if you delve into their history, their language, and their ancient uses. Vegetables will hardly claim your attention throughout the year, unless you are mad for tomatoes-that-taste-like-tomatoes in winter. But if you grow vegetables outdoors, you will surely want to give many of them an indoor start in the greenhouse.

Recommendations for the culture of the plants mentioned, and for many more, are in Part III of this book. As for orchids, they are my own particular hobby, and I devote the rest of this chapter to telling you of the fun I have with them.

42. Fancy-leaved geranium 'Miss Burdett Coutts'. A definite delight in your garden under glass, geraniums bloom and bloom, furnishing great variety of color and form constantly. (MERRY GARDENS PHOTO)

ORCHIDS ARE MY HOBBY

If it were possible to have *one* favorite kind of greenhouse plant, mine would surely be orchids. What other plants are so easy to grow and so spectacular in results? It has always puzzled me that orchids are often thought to be difficult to grow. Cattelya orchids were among the first plants I grew and they continue to give me pleasure year after year. Many greenhouse gardeners have made the same discovery, and today orchids are *everybody's* flowers, appreciated by hobby gardeners the world over. (See Color Plates I, II, VIII.)

Orchid habitats extend from the arctic to the tropics, so it is possible to grow one kind or another whether you have a cool, a moderate, or a warm greenhouse. My night temperature range is 48 to 54 F; the cool and intermediate orchids do just fine, and occasionally even a heat-loving dendrobium has surprised me with bloom. The point is that in a cool greenhouse you can find areas of considerable warmth, just as in a cold outdoor garden there are warmer microclimates where heat-loving plants thrive north of their natural zone. Except for a small group, the requirement of high humidity for orchids is more myth than truth. Relative humidity ranges from 40 to 70 per cent in my greenhouse, the high point being reached only immediately after I have watered plants.

Under my conditions, many orchids thrive—cattleyas, green-leaved cymbidiums, deciduous dendrobiums, reed-stemmed epidendrums, and various others. The heat-loving mottled-leaf cypripediums, the evergreen dendrobiums, and the vandas would be doubtful, though perhaps with extra daily mistings and a location above the heater, they too might perform well.

Orchids offer a vast variety of flower types and plant forms. If you are familiar only with the florist's purple cattleya flower used in corsages, you will be surprised to see the small yellow blooms of *Epidendrum Stamfordianum,* fifty or more to a scape, and they are fragrant, too. The pendent scapes of *Dendrobium aggregatum* are a veritable fountain of yellow, sometimes with more than a hundred 1-inch blossoms on a mature plant. Cypripediums (the native lady-slipper orchids are various hardy species of *Cypripedium,* so you may already be acquainted with this orchid genus) bear large solitary flowers, often 6 inches across, in a wide range of color; and what plant can surpass *Coelogyne cristata* with a dozen or more large, cascading, snow-white blooms, the throats stained a vibrant orange-yellow?

Orchid flowers remain fresh on the plants for weeks—a handsome sight, indeed; but out-of-bloom orchid plants are not much to look at and you may not want them prominently displayed. In the small greenhouse, it is a good idea to grow one each of half a dozen or so different kinds that will give you fall, winter, and spring bloom; or else settle on more plants of just a couple of kinds for an emphatic effect in one season. At the end of this chapter is a list of a dozen easy-to-grow orchids to give you flowers through the year, even in summer if your greenhouse is a year-round affair.

Orchids are certainly fun to grow. From the time you buy your first plant to the day its first blossom opens fully, you are fascinated by the various stages of development. By all means start with mature plants purchased in bud so that almost immediately you can enjoy the color, form, and texture of unfolding flowers. Later, if orchids become your obsession—as well they may—you could grow some from seed. In that case, be prepared to wait five to seven years for bloom!

Epiphytic and terrestrial orchids

There are two basic types of orchids: epiphytic (a plant that grows *upon,* but does not receive its nourishment *from,* another plant, such as a tree), like the familiar cattleya orchid; and terrestrial (a plant that lives and grows in soil), like the spray-type cymbidium orchids. In each type you have a wide choice of plants that will thrive under pretty much the same conditions of heat and humidity. When you buy plants (and this will be mainly from mail-order specialists), find out whether they are epiphytic or terrestrial so you can handle them accordingly.

In nature, epiphytic orchids establish themselves by their fleshy roots on branches or bark of trees. Organic matter that accumulates between the roots and branches furnishes nutrients. There are also some species that cling to rocks for survival. Suspended from trees or on lofty rocks, the epiphytes dwell in filtered light and always in open, airy situations. Some also accommodate themselves to extremes of torrential rain and extended drought. To produce their exotic blooms in profusion in your greenhouse, the epiphytes need to find there an approximation of their natural conditions, particularly in regard to light and air. It is also claimed that a period of dryness between the months of growing and blooming is essential for flowers. However, I have never dried out my cattleyas and oncidiums and, except in dull weather, I water these almost every other day. I do not claim this is ideal practice for *all* epiphytic orchids, but it has certainly worked for these two, which bloom profusely for me on this schedule.

Roots of epiphytic orchids are constructed to sustain the plants through wet and dry periods. The tough, stringy, fiberlike core is encased in a spongy off-white covering that is highly water absorbent. When it rains, this cover soaks up water; when saturated, it turns light green. Roots retain moisture and release it gradually to plant tissues.

The terrestrial, or earth-bound, orchids have roots that grow beneath the surface of the soil, as with most other kinds of plants. Cypripediums, the lady-slipper orchids, are mainly of this type, though some are semi-terrestrial, having both underground and aerial roots.

PLATE I   All in the author's greenhouse: Above, left, snapdragons; right, cyclamens.

Above, left, gloxinias; right, lilies. Below, left, *Epidendrum ibaguense;* right, cinerarias and cyclamens.

PLATE II   Above, left, *Tulbaghia violacea;* right, oxalis.

Above, left, cattleya orchids; right, *Veltheimia viridifolia.* Below, left, Saint-paulia 'Lilian Jarrett' (TINARI PHOTO); right, tibouchina.

PLATE III   Above, left, abutilon; right, *Ophthalmophyllum Herrei* (KALM-
BACHER PHOTO).

Above, left, *Senecio Petasitis;* right, *Cestrum aurantiacum.* Below, left,
Crassula 'Morgans Pink'; right, Aporophyllum 'Temple Fire' (KALMBACHER
PHOTOS).

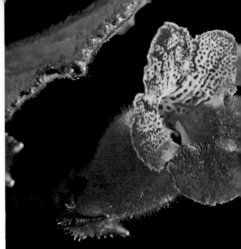

PLATE IV   Above, left, *Acalypha hispida;* right, *Kohleria eriantha.*

Above, left, *Lobivia Backebergii* (KALMBACHER PHOTO); right, haemanthus. Below, left, kalanchoe; right, Rhipsalidopsis 'Crimson Giant' (KALMBACHER PHOTO).

PLATE V Above: Early fall chrysanthemums are prolific and colorful. Below: This even-span greenhouse makes a pleasing addition to the outdoor garden.

PLATE VI Opposite page: A collection of many kinds of geraniums affords year-round pleasure in a hobby greenhouse. (ROCHE PHOTO)

PLATE VII Above: Combine a living-room with your gardening hobby in this attractive manner.

PLATE VIII   Above: Try miltonias, oncidiums, and cattleyas for an interesting collection of orchids. (GENEREUX PHOTO). Below: Tulips, hyacinths, and azaleas defy winter weather.

The lovely spray orchids, cymbidiums, are terrestrial; they grow in the loose humus of rotted wood or decayed leaves.

Types of growth

Orchids are further classified as to type of growth. The familiar cattleya grows from a horizontal rhizome that sends out roots from below and a "lead" each year from above. The lead curves gradually upward to an erect leathery growth from which a flower bud emerges. The lower part of the lead enlarges to form a pseudobulb and a leaf emerges at this point. Such orchids are known as sympodial or "feet together" and this is the more common type.

The monopodial or one-footed orchids include the vandas and angraecums. With these, a stem extends upward and leaves develop alternately along it. The flower spikes emerge from the leaf axils.

Then there are orchids, such as the dendrobiums, that are further classified as evergreen or deciduous. For example, *Dendrobium nobile* drops leaves from its reedy pseudobulbs about the middle of the second year and flowers then appear along the almost leafless stems. The evergreen cane-type *Dendrobium thyrsiflorum* retains its broad fleshy leaves and produces handsome white clusters of orange-tipped flowers from the tops of the canes.

Heat, light, and humidity

For greenhouse growing, orchids should be selected and grouped according to their more-or-less definite requirements of heat and light. As I have said, most of the more demanding high-temperature, high-humidity species can be accommodated somewhere in the cool or moderate greenhouse. Few require full sun; most do well in filtered sunshine or bright light. In winter, I place my orchids in the lightest possible locations in the greenhouse; in summer, light is filtered through slats or vinyl shading. (If you have an outdoor garden, you can suspend the plants from tree branches during summer.) During summer in the greenhouse, high humidity is essential and this is provided by frequent wetting down of walks and under-bench areas; of course, a mist system is ideal in hot weather, and also in winter for the high-humidity group. A good circulation of air is essential in every season.

The orchid fancier will find that benches, built in stepped-up tiers with an area of coke or gravel below, are ideal for growing and display. From the frequently water-sprinkled coke or gravel, moisture evaporates to surround the plants with welcome humidity, and the open placement in tiers assures a fine circulation of air.

In the small greenhouse, orchids are usually set on benches filled with sand or gravel but raised a little on a wire-mesh covering or on slatted sections made of half-inch redwood strips. Humidity and air circulation around roots are thus provided. If you are growing just a few orchid plants, I can also recommend the simple arrangement of placing the plants on inverted flower pots.

Culture for the various types of orchids differs somewhat but it is surprising how accommodating most of them can be. In fact, once they are established, it is not at all difficult to bring plants to maturity with minimum effort. Most specialists include directions with their plants, and new potting materials have further simplified culture.

Potting, watering, and feeding

Formerly only osmunda fiber was recommended as a potting material; it required tedious soaking and packing of the pot. Today there is readily available the economical white firbark. It comes in graded sizes, is easy to handle, and is suitable for potting the epiphytic orchids, including the rock-growers. In firbark the growth is vigorous and circulation of air around the roots is assured. I have also successfully grown small plants of the terrestrial type in firbark, but they can be potted in the same soil mixture you use for your other plants.

Potting with firbark alone is a simple matter in the special orchid pots that have large drainage holes. First fill the pot about one-third up with broken crock. This is particularly important if seedling-size grade of firbark is used—without sufficient crocking, this will wash through the big drainage holes. Position the plant in the pot with roots spread out over the crocking. Then fill in with firbark to within an inch of the top while you firm the bark around the roots with your thumbs, just as you do when potting plants in soil. Water well to settle the bark. This will hold the plant erect while you stake it, if this is necessary. In any case, pot securely; wobbly plants do not thrive.

After a few weeks, orchids in firbark alone require frequent watering until the bark has become well saturated. The epiphytes with aerial roots *and* pseudobulbs—cattleys and odontoglossums—while requiring a certain amount of moist air around the roots need to dry out somewhat between waterings. Phalaenopsis and other monopodial orchids that do not have pseudobulbs, as vandas and cypripediums, are watered enough to keep the potting medium damp but not soaked.

Terrestrial and semi-terrestrial orchids—cypripediums and cymbidiums—require abundant moisture, but there must be good drainage to prevent sogginess. Mine are watered thoroughly every other day throughout the year, except during rainy periods; then, especially in winter, I skip an extra day or two, depending on the duration of the dull, wet weather.

Firbark is deficient in nitrogen, so feeding is essential. Apply any soluble orchid plant-food or fish emulsion as the manufacturer's directions indicate. With the exception of cymbidiums, orchids seem to require less nourishment than other plants, and on this account dilute applications of fertilizer are often advised.

Repotting and dividing orchids

I hesitated to use firbark when it became necessary to repot my larger cymbidiums, which are, of course, terrestrial orchids. I noticed that they had originally been potted by the grower in a medium with considerably more substance to it. Therefore I tried a mixture of equal parts of sand, firbark, and shredded osmunda fiber, and apparently hit upon a good combination for my older plants thrive and bloom freely in this.

Need for repotting will usually be quite apparent. Roots will push out of drainage holes or extend over the tops of pots. Once plants are established in fairly large pots, say 6's or 8's, it will not be necessary to repot for two or three years. Then large plants should be divided.

Mature orchids with pseudobulbs—cattleyas and laelias—should be split with a sharp knife. Cut through the rhizome leaving at least three and preferably four pseudobulbs to each section. Get rid of any dead roots and worn-out potting material. If one or two roots have grown very long, cut them back; you will not injure the plant. Put the sections in individual pots with the heel of the pseudobulb about half an inch from the wall of the pot. Use pots large enough to allow room for the development of two to three leads before the next repotting. For repotting, use firbark or my firbark-sand-osmunda fiber mixture.

Handle cypripediums a little differently. Cut the plant into pieces, each with at least one bit of growth. Repot in a mixture of equal parts of osmunda fiber, sand, and leafmold, for these orchids are of the terrestrial type.

Propagate the evergreen dendrobiums by offsets, those tiny plants that develop their own root systems while still a part of the parent plant. With the deciduous dendrobiums—whose pseudobulbs bloom only once and can now be cut out of the plant—make 3- to 5-inch sections each containing a node or two. Spread these out in moist sand in

43. An orchid hobbyist would be delighted with this greenhouse full of phalaenopsis, cattleya, and oncidium orchids in full bloom. (GOTTSCHO-SCHLEISNER PHOTO)

a warm, humid place, where small plants will form in a few weeks. When they have developed a good root system, cut them apart and plant individually in small pots. The thin wiry root systems do not need large pots, even when plants are mature.

Few troubles

Orchids are remarkably free of pests and disease. Only once in five years did I have trouble. Aphids appeared on one plant but I hand-cleaned it and saw no more. If you put cymbidiums outdoors in summer, watch out for snails and slugs, and be sure to inspect in fall before pots are returned to the greenhouse, especially if you placed them on the ground under bushes or trees. Tiny soil flies appear occasionally, but they seem to do no damage and disappear of their own accord.

If your plants are troubled enough that spraying or fumigation is required, be sure to check materials for safety on orchids. Orchids do not tolerate certain chemicals and a treatment with one of those could be more damaging than an infestation.

Some viruses attack orchid plants; it would be unfair to lead you to believe there could be no trouble from that source. However, if you always maintain good air circulation, especially in a greenhouse with high humidity, your virus problems will be few, if any.

In any case, don't be afraid of orchids. Most of them are very easy to grow and so spectacular in bloom that they are more rewarding than most other plants. In a word, orchids are fun!

A DOZEN EASY ORCHIDS FOR SUCCESSION OF BLOOM
(*Night temperature 50 to 55 F*)

Orchid	Flower color	Flower season	Plant height in inches
Oncidium tigrinum splendidum	yellow and brown	winter, spring	12 to 18
Lycaste aromatica	yellow	winter	10 to 16

Epidendrum atropur-pureum	greenish-brown tinged with purple	spring	16 to 24
Cattleya Skinneri	rose-purple	spring	12 to 26
Brassavola nodosa	white	various	6 to 9
Epidendrum × O'Briena-num	red, pink, or orange	spring, summer	24 to 62
Dendrobium densiflorum	orange-yellow	spring	20 to 36
Odontoglossum grande	yellow and brown	winter	10 to 16
Phaius grandifolius	brown and white	summer	22 to 40
Trichopilia tortilis	pink, white lip	spring, summer	8 to 12
Stanhopea Wardii	yellow or white, spotted purple	late summer	24 to 36
Oncidium ampliatum	golden yellow	early spring	10 to 20

13

Vegetables and Herbs

It might be fun, from the standpoint of variety, to devote some of your greenhouse area to a few vegetables and herbs; and practical, too, if you like bright red, summer-type tomatoes during the bleak days of winter, and gourmet seasonings for salads and stews.

VEGETABLES

The number and kinds of vegetables you grow is limited only by the amount of space you wish to devote to them and by the temperature requirements of the individual crops. Cultural directions are much the same for all: a rich, fibrous well-drained soil, though root crops such as carrots, beets, and radishes shape up better and are smoother in texture if a good bit of sand is worked into the soil mixture. They all like plenty of sun, and this is especially important when they are grown in winter under glass. Keep vegetables well watered after seedlings have been transplanted to their permanent locations, and a humid atmosphere is beneficial. A regular feeding every two to three weeks with a complete liquid fertilizer is important during periods of active growth.

Tomatoes will probably be your first choice, and one or two plants grown in large pots will undoubtedly be enough. If plantings are staggered over several weeks, you will have tomatoes available until well into spring, but the first sowing must be in July since fruit will ripen in a 60 F temperature only if it is well set on the vines before the short days of fall. Grow the plant to a single stem, staked for support. To assure that fruit will set, pollinate blossoms by hand, shake vines to fertilize the blossoms, or use a hormone-type tomato spray on the blossoms. I found it a simple matter to hand pollinate with an artist's small red-sable brush. 'Tuckcross O.' is a vigorous hybrid with smooth, meaty fruit, specially recommended for greenhouse forcing. You might try one of the small-fruit tomatoes, such as 'Tiny Tim', 15 inches tall with ¾-inch tomatoes with a fine flavor; or 'Patio' with medium-sized fruit on a 2-foot vine (this one was developed for growing in limited space).

Bibb lettuce is an excellent companion for tomatoes, requiring the same 60 F temperature. Sow every two weeks from the first of September for a winter and spring crop, and transplant from the germinating medium directly into the bench, 6 to 8 inches apart. Give plenty of water. Try 'Bibb Forcing', 'Burpee Bibb' or 'Butter King' for well-formed heads of tender, tasty lettuce; or 'Grand Rapids Forcing' for a loose-leaf variety.

Radishes add crisp color to your winter salads if you have a growing area that will hold a 50 F temperature. 'Cherry Belle' is an extra-early variety. Make successive sowings from late September on, in a light and sandy soil. Do not crowd.

Beets can be grown in a cool house, at 45 to 50 F. Plant about 3 inches apart in rows spaced 6 inches apart, and use when half-grown for best flavor. Tops are tasty as a cooked vegetable, too. Try 'Detroit Dark Red', 'Short Top', or 'Lutz Green Leaf'; 'Winter Keeper' takes a little longer to mature but is popular for its greens.

Carrots grown in the greenhouse should be selected from such varieties as Burpee's 'Goldinhart' or 'Chantenay'—tender, sweet, and only about 5½ inches long when fully mature. Other varieties may be selected if they are used when half-mature (benches do not have sufficient depth to grow 7- or 8-inch roots). When forced for winter use, carrots need a temperature of 50 F with bottom heat for best growth.

Cucumbers may be grown under glass but they require a temperature of 70 F to germinate and at least 65 F to grow. You might try them if you plan to use your greenhouse all summer, and they can be started as early as the first of March under glass. 'Ball Early Hybrid' is an excellent variety for greenhouse growing.

No matter what your favorite vegetable may be, those grown under glass can be picked at the peak of maturity, preferably just before using, for a fresher, sweeter flavor. And the fact that you can have them out of season makes them doubly enjoyable.

HERBS

Your greenhouse provides an excellent opportunity to grow your own herbs. And nothing adds spice to your life, or to your salads and stews, like a bit of flavorful chive or basil picked fresh from your garden. Turn the everyday boredom of cooking into an interesting and exciting adventure and at the same time add delicate blossoms and aromatic fragrance to your garden.

Most herbs do well under glass. They require plenty of sunshine and temperatures upwards from 50 F. Humidity is beneficial, and a soil mixture of equal parts sand, peatmoss, garden loam, and well-rotted manure provides the nourishment and good drainage needed for optimum growth. Provide good air circulation and syringe the plants occasionally to remove accumulated or splashed dust or dirt—cleanliness is essential if herbs are to be used in cooking. Pests are few, but if trouble develops, select your control material carefully, mindful that many sprays or dusts must not be used on plants that are to be eaten.

Young plants may be purchased from garden centers or mail-order houses in spring or fall, or you may try your hand at raising your favorite from seed which may be planted just about any time you wish.

If you have never used herbs in cooking, you have a delightful treat in store. There is no end to the possibilities. Some herbs are more delicate than others, and you will have to experiment a bit before arriving at the right amount to suit your individual taste. Most leaves are dried before being used, but some, such as parsley or mint, are used fresh as a garnish as well as dried. Chive has a delicate onion-flavored foliage that is cut as needed for soups or salads. Dill leaves are used to flavor sauces or pickles. Some herbs have medicinal properties: anise is steeped as a tea to treat colic, catnip tea aids digestion, horehound leaves steeped in boiling water provide a cough remedy.

Follow suggestions in cookbooks or cooking columns as a start. Then branch out on your own—experiment, be adventurous. There's no limit to the fun and interest to be found in a tiny herb garden in your greenhouse.

ANISE (*Pimpinella Anisum*). Annual, height 1 foot, white flowers. Seeds and leaves used for flavoring, leaves for garnishes.

BASIL (*Ocimum Basilicum*). Annual, height about 1 foot. Use leaves to season soups, meats, salads, cheese souffle, omelets, or in a cheese-dip.

CARAWAY (*Carum Carvi*). Annual or biennial, height 1 foot. Use seeds in breads, cakes, or to flavor cheese.

CHIVE (*Allium Schoenoprasum*). Tender green leaves are cut and used fresh to give a delicate onion flavor to soups, salads, and soft cheeses.

DILL (*Anethum graveolens*). Annual or biennial to 2 feet tall; yellow flowers. Use leaves to flavor pickles and sauces.

FENNEL (*Foeniculum vulgare*). A perennial best grown as an annual because plants reach 4 feet in height. Use the leaves dried to flavor fish sauces, and green for garnishing.

LEMON BALM (*Melissa officinalis*). Annual, about a foot tall. Use leaves to season soups, meats, salads.

ROSEMARY (*Rosmarinus officinalis*). Hardy evergreen that grows to 3 feet, has spikes of pale blue flowers. Prefers an alkaline soil. Leaves are delicious in chicken soup, ham-loaf, cauliflower, or cooked with potatoes before mashing.

SUMMER SAVORY (*Satureja annua*). Annual, about 18 inches tall. Sprinkle the aromatic leaves in consomme or split-pea soup, or combine them with hash or scrambled eggs.

SWEET MARJORAM (*Majorana hortensis*). Annual, sweet flowers on 2-foot spikes. Use leaves for seasoning: in chicken soup, combined with thyme to dust chicken before frying, or sprinkled on fish fillets before cooking.

TARRAGON (*Artemisia Dracunculus*). Perennial, grows to 2 feet in height. Cook dried leaves with beets, sprinkle on fish fillets, or combine with flour for dusting liver before cooking.

THYME (*Thymus vulgaris*). Low-growing evergreen, only 6 inches high. Use dried leaves for seasoning.

WINTER SAVORY (*Satureja montana*). Evergreen plant with dwarf characteristics, lilac flowers. Dried leaves used for seasonings and flavor.

14

How to Increase Your Plants

Plants are increased by two basic methods—seeds or vegetative reproduction. Vegetative propagation (*propagation* is the word usually used by gardeners to describe the process of creating new plants) includes several different methods by which parts of living plants other than seed are used to produce new plants. Plants propagated by vegetative means are duplicates of, and have exactly the same characteristics as, the parent plant. Seedlings, which are completely new plants, may or may not be like the parent; plants (called hybrids) from seeds resulting from a cross between two different plants may resemble either or neither parent or inherit one or more characteristics from both parents. Vegetative methods of reproduction include *cuttings*—leaf, stem, or root; *division*—of a large plant, or of a tuber, corm, rhizome, bulb, or roots; and *layering*. Budding and grafting are other methods of vegetative propagation of new plants from old, but they are a bit tricky and usually practiced only by experienced gardeners. There is nothing difficult or mysterious about any of this, and knowing how and why it is better to use one propagating method instead of another for each kind of plant makes the whole thing fun rather than just another task.

GROWING PLANTS FROM SEEDS

Seeds offer just about the easiest and least expensive way to obtain quantities of new plants. Nature most commonly produces new plants by seed, and plants raised from seeds are often more robust and less susceptible to disease than plants produced by a vegetative reproduction method. Many kinds of plants needed for spring and summer outdoor gardens, such as snapdragons, zinnias, marigolds, stocks, asters, and petunias, and many greenhouse plants like calceolaria, cineraria, schizanthus, primrose, and cyclamen are usually grown from seed. It is the only method of producing the annuals and biennials that flower, seed, and die in either one or two years. Most vegetables are raised from seed each year.

Seed harvested from our own plants cannot always be depended upon to produce the results we'd like. Seed from a parent that is itself a spectacular hybrid often produces unworthy or very ordinary plants. We should obtain our seed from reliable sources, that is, from seedsmen who are experts—dealers who test their seeds and offer only the very best strains and varieties. Only the best quality seed is worth sowing. You must be assured of good germination so your time and effort will not be wasted.

But before you start buying those entrancing packets of seed, may I offer the voice of experience: make haste slowly. While your greenhouse is being put up, doubtlessly you are dreaming of benches bulging, shelves overflowing, and your greenhouse literally bursting with your favorite flowers: sweet-scented stock, stately delphinium, clouds of baby's-breath, gorgeous fuchsias, and baskets of trailing ivy-leaved geraniums and *Campanula isophylla*. Eventually your dream can come true—but not right off. Packets hold hundreds of tiny seeds, and if you grow even half a dozen kinds, you may find yourself with a multitude of seedlings all needing to be transplanted at the same time. Nothing is so frustrating or time-consuming, nothing more discouraging! So start small: the years ahead will give you the opportunity to try everything you admire.

Sterile mediums for seeds

Your method of sowing seeds will be determined largely by what you intend to do with the mature plants. If they are for the outdoor garden, enough will be needed to justify the use of large seed flats. If the plants are for the greenhouse, you will want a smaller quantity, and small fiber flats will be adequate.

You can sow seeds in one of the sterile mediums that you can buy, and this is an easy way to do it; or you can prepare a special soil mixture. However, you will get excellent results from sowings in milled sphagnum moss, vermiculite, or perlite. No harmful fungi are present

44. SEED PLANTING IS EASY. Fill flat with sterile planting medium, mark off rows, sow seeds, label. Tags with brief cultural directions are helpful when several kinds of seeds are being grown for the first time.

in these and all are moisture retentive; seedlings are easily transplanted from them without disturbance to delicate root systems, for the material clings to make a little clump around each tiny network of roots. However, plant food must be provided *soon after* seedlings poke through, as these sterile mediums contain practically no plant nourishment.

Milled (pulverized and sifted) *sphagnum moss* is a superb seed-bed material. The danger of damp-off—that dreaded fungous disease that causes infant plants to collapse and rot—is minimized, for drainage is excellent and substantial root growth occurs.

Vermiculite is composed of expanded mica flakes that are very light in weight, yet retain moisture evenly and allow good air circulation for roots. Be sure to get the small-particled horticultural vermiculite; you don't want the coarse, treated type that is used for insulation because it may be toxic to plants, as some gardeners have learned to their sorrow.

Perlite is exploded lava, a white, glass-like silica derivative that weighs about one-tenth as much as sand. It has a slightly acid reaction but not enough to bother most plants.

Sand mixed with peatmoss or sphagnum is good for seed sowing, also, but as with other sterile mediums, plant food is eventually required. Sand by itself won't do for sowing seeds, because it lets water run right through and does not retain the moisture that is needed.

Soil mixtures for seeds

You can prepare a light, loose soil mixture of your own. In this the tiny hairlike roots of new seedlings can easily work their way through and absorb the nourishment necessary for their development. Equal amounts of coarse sand, peatmoss or leafmold, and soil, make a good mix. If your soil is on the sandy side, you will find that two parts soil, two parts peatmoss or leafmold, and only one part sand will make a better growing medium than the equal thirds.

Sterilize your soil mixture or drench it with a fungicide to prevent damp-off of seedlings. Spores of this fungous disease apparently are present in all soils, and the moisture necessary for germination of seed and growth of seedlings provides the ideal condition for development of the fungus. Damp-off is practically impossible to control once it gets started in a seed-bed. Surgically clean tools and equipment are essential; drafts and sudden changes in temperature are to be avoided.

Add no fertilizer to your soil mixture. Seeds contain the nutrients to carry them through to germination.

Sowing the seeds

Prepare flats for sowing by spreading about half an inch of coarse sand or unmilled sphagnum moss over the bottom. Then fill to within a quarter-inch of the top with the medium you have chosen. Place the flat in a vessel of water until enough moisture is drawn up by capillary action to moisten the top soil. This will help to firm the medium into a flat bed for sowing and also make it properly moist but not sopping wet. Then fill to the top of the flat with more of the medium which has been screened through a fine sieve or a piece of quarter-inch hardware cloth. With a trowel, the edge of a ruler, or a piece of lath, mark off planting rows, about 2 inches apart. Sow the seeds shallowly in the rows, covering them with sieved soil to a depth of about twice their thickness, no more. Pat the rows lightly to firm them.

It is easier to broadcast the very fine seeds of petunias, snapdragons, begonias, lobelias, gloxinias and other gesneriads over the whole surface of the flat than to sow in rows, and these fine ones need no covering of soil. Or you can buy "pelleted" seeds of the very tiny kinds. These have a coating that protects from disease and also contains food. Pelleted seeds germinate quickly and, being larger, are easier to sow thinly, thus avoiding crowded bunched seedlings. They require special handling, so follow the directions that come with them.

Large seeds, such as those of nasturtiums, or the hard seeds of sweet-peas and morning-glories, seem to germinate more readily if soaked overnight in warm water before planting. You can nick the hard ones with a sharp knife, but I never found this very easy to do. You may prefer to plant larger seeds in peat pots filled with your medium. Insert one or two seeds per pot, water well, and stand the pots on a shelf above the heater to give bottom heat which promotes germination. When seedlings are well developed, transfer to a bench of soil, to standard pots, or plant directly in the garden with no intervening transplanting. Peat pots provide some nourishment and usually disintegrate in the bench or in the ground when roots penetrate the pot walls.

If you prefer, you can sow all your seeds in standard pots, bulb-pans, glass kitchen casseroles, or even in egg shells. Prepare pots by covering each drainage hole with an arched piece of clay pot ("crock" or "potshard," as these pieces are sometimes called) to prevent soil from washing out. To keep soil sweet in deep pots, spread a little horticultural charcoal over the bottom before filling in the planting medium.

As you finish with each packet of seed, label the flat or pot. Write the name of the plant and the date of sowing on each marker, also something about culture if there is room. Use a waterproof marking pencil so your identification won't disappear. You will be surprised how much alike seedlings look until the first true leaves (usually the second set of leaves) appear. If you sow more than one kind of seed in a flat, label each row.

Water the sowings lightly with a hand bulb-spray or mist bottle. Then cover the flats with a piece of glass to retain humidity, and spread newspaper over the glass, since many seeds seem to germinate best in darkness. Or slip the well-watered flat into a large plastic bag; or cover the flat with a sheet of plastic tucked under on all sides. This way, soil stays evenly moist and the glass or plastic helps maintain an even temperature. Translucent plastic is best because it shades sowings, but clear plastic could be covered with paper.

To make seed sowing almost foolproof, there are seed-starter kits that include everything you need: peat flats, peat pots, sphagnum moss, soil heating cable, labels, marking pencil, plastic bags, even a handbook of advice. I like to use these kits and have had excellent results with them. I soak the sphagnum moss until it absorbs a quantity of water, then squeeze it gently to remove the excess water, but not hard enough to pack it; then rub it gently between my fingers as I fill the flat. Seeds are sprinkled on top of the sphagnum with no covering for fine ones and just a sprinkling of sphagnum for larger ones. The seed flat, slipped into a plastic bag with the end folded over, is set in a somewhat shaded location until germination occurs.

Propagating case

An excellent way to handle seeds or cuttings is to convert a bench section into a propagating case. With boards, partition off an area of bench. Place a section of glass, perhaps a discarded window frame, on top, supported by the framework of wood. Or more simply, tack a piece of translucent plastic along the back of the bench and roll it forward

45. PROPAGATING CASE. One end of a bench is converted to a propagating case by filling a partitioned area with sand, vermiculite, or perlite. Provide a flexible plastic cover to roll over the area to retain humidity.

over the area you have seeded. For cuttings, prop up the plastic with clothes pins or wire coat hangers to keep it from touching the plants.

Care of seedlings

Inspect your sowings daily. As soon as seedlings appear, remove the covering. Expose seedlings to light and *gradually* to full sun. Keep in mind that they are tender; too much sun immediately after germination lets moisture evaporate from leaves more rapidly than tiny roots can replace it to the plant. Seedlings may not survive such exposure. Most seeds of the same kind germinate about the same time and when a fair number of seedlings appear, the plastic is removed. There will be a few late-comers but these will not be unduly affected by removal of the cover. Do not wait for complete germination or you will have too many leggy seedlings that will not grow into strong plants.

As germination occurs, you will notice that even the best seed sown most carefully produces some seedlings that seem more vigorous than others. Although your inclination may be to nurse the weaklings, it is usually wise to discard them. Thinning out the unfit lets in more light and air to strengthen the others. Try to cull the weaklings without disturbing roots of the strong ones. A good way is to snip or pinch the weak plants out close to the soil. (However, with experience you will discover that in some cases, as with highly developed strains of, say, delphiniums, it is the apparent weaklings that later produce handsome plants of particularly fine color, but that is not your concern now.)

Transplanting seedlings

It is important to keep the seedlings growing and not to let them remain overlong in the germinating medium. Root systems develop rapidly and if they get too large they are easily damaged in transplanting. Move seedlings when the first true leaves appear. You can usually see the difference between the first and second sets of leaves. If you are in doubt about the second set, wait for the third, but then delay no longer. You can transplant directly into a greenhouse bench, into other seed flats, or into pots, depending upon how you intend to use your plants. Let them go a little dry for several days beforehand; then water well just before shifting. Moist soil clings better than dry soil to tiny roots.

If you plan direct benching, prepare a well-aerated soil rich in humus; this will stimulate vigorous root development. With a dibble or

46. TRANSPLANTING IS EASY when you set up an assembly line. Prepare the pots, separate seedlings by pulling them apart gently, center each seedling in a pot (supporting it with one hand while the other hand fills in and around with soil), and mist gently to settle soil firmly around roots.

pencil, make about 2-inch-deep indentations in regular rows, spacing the indents according to directions on seed packets. If space is at a premium in your greenhouse—not an unusual condition—put plants a little closer than recommended. Just keep in mind that it is important for sunlight and air to reach each seedling.

When your seedlings have been well watered and allowed to stand while you prepare the bench soil for them, they are ready for transplanting. Be gentle, work slowly, first plant the areas farthest from you —across the bench nearest the glass. Then work forward, row by row.

To remove seedlings from the seed-bed, use any handy item: dibble, pencil, orangewood stick, or plastic fork. Press the tool down to the side and slightly behind each seedling, and with a scooping upward motion lift it up supported between thumb and forefinger. If seedlings are too tiny to handle in this manner, lift them with tweezers. Lower the rooted seedling into the prepared hole and to the same depth it stood in the flat; hold it steady while you firmly press soil around it. Take care not to bend roots; rather, suspend them into holes that are big enough for them. When all seedlings have been transplanted, water them thoroughly but gently to settle soil compactly about the roots.

Cover the transplants with newspapers or translucent plastic for a few days to protect from direct sun until they have become established in their new quarters. When it is evident that growth continues, remove the covering and give an application of liquid fertilizer. Repeat at two-week intervals. Fish emulsion, diluted according to directions, is excellent for transplanted seedlings.

If you are moving seedlings to a flat, work the same way as for bench planting but save time by making a number of holes at once with the dibble board described in Chapter 4. Spacing on the dibble board will be for plants of average size; if your seedlings are fairly large, set them in every other space instead of in each space.

You can water flats by sub-irrigation. Set the flat in a large container of water until the soil absorbs enough to feel moist on top. Then promptly remove the flat from the water. Sub-irrigation assures even distribution of moisture without wetting the foliage, which sometimes encourages disease.

NEW PLANTS FROM CUTTINGS, DIVISION, LAYERING

An easy way to increase your supply of plants is to grow new ones from cuttings, that is, from pieces of the plant you have. Almost any part of the plant is a possibility—leaf, root, or stem—but some parts work better for some plants than for others. Stem or softwood cuttings work well for geraniums, begonias, fuchsias, chrysanthemums, carnations, and many other plants. You can propagate azaleas, camellias, roses, and jasmine from stem pieces called hardwood cuttings. Leaf cuttings are good for begonias and African-violets, and root cuttings for poppies, *Anemone japonica*, gaillardia, and Oriental poppies.

In no other greenhouse operation is cleanliness more important than with cuttings. Obviously, it is essential to take cuttings only from disease-free plants, and then to use only spotlessly clean tools and materials. Even though you plant in a sterile medium and dip cuttings into a hormone powder containing a fungicide, keep in mind that the knife you use, the bench on which you lay cuttings, even your hands, can carry disease to the open end of a cutting. It is a good idea to dip the cutting knife in a solution of laundry bleach between each cut.

To propagate from cuttings, select what we might call middle-aged growth. Very young tips do not have adequate reserves to produce rooted plants soon enough to resist a possible fungous attack. Old growth may have hardened past the root-producing stage and, again, cuttings from it may not be able to produce a root system in time for survival. What you want is the healthy, vigorous plant material that develops midway in the growth cycle of the plant.

How to make softwood and hardwood cuttings

Try your hand first with softwood cuttings of, perhaps, geraniums. These are so easy to propagate from stem cuttings. Select firm, 3- to 4-inch-long tip pieces with at least three sets of leaves. Cut with a sharp knife straight across the stem and just below a node, that little joint on the stem from which leaves start to grow. Take care not to bruise stem tissues as you cut. Strip off the lower leaves and also all flowers and buds. Let some leaves remain, say two or three, to nourish the new plant.

To speed things up, dip the cut ends in a hormone powder like Rootone or Hormodin, but be sure to shake off excess powder before planting. These rooting agents contain a fungicide that protects cuttings from rotting; they are most useful when the rooting medium has not been sterilized.

Fill the flat or cutting bed with sharp sand or a mixture of sand and peatmoss or sphagnum moss. Insert cuttings deep enough to support them but don't let any leaves touch the rooting medium. Firm each cutting securely. Provide bottom heat with a lead-covered heating cable or just set the flat on a shelf above the heater. Cover cuttings with plastic to maintain soil moisture and promote the humidity that encourages quick rooting. Shade for a few days with plastic or newspaper. Lift this while you mist the cuttings with a fine water spray perhaps once or twice a day.

Hardwood cuttings are set deeper than softwood, and need more time to root; they also require a little more heat.

Pot-in-pan device

When you have only a few cuttings to propagate, the pot-in-pan device is a convenience. Place a small clay pot, the drainage hole stoppered with a cork or floral clay, in the center of an 8-inch bulb-pan. Fill the area between the pots with clean sharp sand or other rooting medium, soak it well, then insert the cuttings in a circle around the small pot. Fill the center pot with water to the brim. Water will seep through the porous walls of the clay pot to maintain even moisture for the cuttings. The entire arrangement can be covered with a plastic bag to produce a humid atmosphere.

Transplanting rooted cuttings to pots

As a rule, take up cuttings when roots are half an inch long. You can check by gently lifting one cutting and gently putting it back if roots are still too small. Try not to let cuttings remain overlong before transplanting to more spacious quarters and richer soil. It takes only a little experience to get a feeling for the right time. For most transplants the equal-thirds mixture of garden soil, leafmold, and sand is good, with a little extra leafmold for those plants that are developing fine root systems, as African-violets and begonias.

Make the first transfer of rooted cuttings to 2½- or 3-inch pots—nothing smaller because the soil will dry out so quickly you will never have the watering can or hose out of your hand. However, it does help to plunge well-watered small pots into a bench section of sand, vermiculite, or perlite which can then be kept fairly moist, and the moisture will penetrate the walls or clay pots. Still, you must check frequently,

47. CUTTINGS. Stem, root, and leaf cuttings are simple ways to increase favorite plants; hormone powder containing a fungicide helps promote fast rooting. Pot-in-pan device covered with plastic is an ideal method to root cuttings because it supplies and retains needed moisture and humidity.

for too much moisture rots new roots by keeping soil so wet that air cannot enter.

If your clay pots are new, soak them in water for several hours before using because dry clay draws moisture from the soil. I soak old pots overnight in a strong Lysol solution to disinfect them and then rinse well in clean water. If algae and accumulated salts remain, I scrub with a wire brush till pots are clean—sometimes a laborious business.

When many seedlings or cuttings are to be transplanted, an assembly line speeds the work. Set pots in rows on your potting bench. Place a bit of broken pot, a stone, or a little unmilled sphagnum moss or osmunda fiber over the drainage hole in each one to prevent soil from washing through. Scatter over this a small amount of horticultural charcoal to help keep soil sweet. Then fill pots with the planting medium to within a quarter- to half-inch of the top, depending on pot size. Insert a plant in each and water moderately. Once plants are established and growing, start a regular schedule of feeding.

Leaf cuttings

There are two ways to propagate plants from leaves. Short-stemmed leaves of African-violets, some begonias, and various other plants are rooted somewhat the same as stem cuttings. Large leaves, or parts of them, of Rex and other begonias, are laid flat on the rooting medium.

To propagate African-violets, select firm leaves of medium size but not from the oldest, mature ones in the outside ring of growth. Cut sharply with about 1-inch petioles (leaf stems), insert halfway in the rooting medium and firm this well around them. Even so, you may have to prop each leaf up with a plant label until it forms supporting roots. If you are rooting just a few leaves, you can place each in a 2¼-inch pot and cover with a fruit-juice glass or plastic bag, propped on sticks, to insure humidity. The pot-in-pan device is also convenient for African-violets.

Tiny new plants appear at the base of a parent leaf in a few weeks but, unless the parent leaf deteriorates, do not cut it off until there is a sizable cluster of plantlets. When these are about a third the size of the old leaf, you can dispense with it and divide the colony into separate plants. These will usually flower in eight to nine months, sometimes in six.

African-violet leaves also root readily in water. Place a piece of waxed paper or plastic over the top of a glass of water and secure it with a rubber band. Insert one or more leaf stems through small holes in the covering. Suspend them so that only the ends of the stem reach into the water. Add more water as it is needed to keep the water level constant. Roots will soon form and plantlets develop above them. When they are large enough to handle, transfer each leaf with its cluster of plantlets to a small pot. Let the plants become well established before cutting off the parent leaf.

Plants with large, prominently veined leaves, like many of the begonias, are easily propagated from a healthy, well-developed leaf, again middle-aged rather than old or young. Make two or three slashes across the main veins and peg the leaf to the sand or soil mixture with hairpins or toothpicks, or weight it with pebbles. The cut edges must be in contact with the moist mixture. As plantlets develop along the cuts, give light liquid feedings. When the young plants are large enough to handle, cut them apart, each with a bit of root, and transfer to separate small pots or space out in a flat where there is room for development.

Begonias and some other plants can be propagated by V-shaped pieces of leaves, each section having a large vein. Insert the point of the V deep enough in the rooting medium to hold the leaf upright. Small plants will develop around the point.

Layering
If you grow decorative foliage plants such as aralias, dacenas, dieffenbachias, and of course rubber plants, the time will come when these will lose their looks by stretching tall and dropping lower leaves. At this point you·still admire the tops but you find the plant as a whole far from attractive. However, by a method known as layering (actually another means of propagation by stem cutting) you can save the handsome tops and get rid of the bare stems.

With a sharp knife, cut halfway through the stem at the distance from the top that you decide will make an attractive plant. From this crosscut, split the stem upward for about 2 inches, and dust the inside of the cut with a rooting hormone. At the top of the cut, insert a small sterile object, such as a piece of wood or a pebble, to keep the split open, and press a small pad of moist sphagnum moss into the slit. Wrap more moist moss over the wound and around the stem, covering an area of about 2 inches above and below the cut. Cover the moist moss with a plastic wrap to retain moisture, and seal top and bottom of plastic wrap with tape or tie with plastic plant ties.

The root system that develops from the cut will penetrate the moss and be visible through the plastic covering. When roots appear adequate to sustain the top growth, remove plastic and moss. Just below the rootball, cut through the stem of the parent plant and pot up the new plant. If you cut back the lower part of the old plant to about 2 inches it may send out new shoots and you will have two plants. With dieffenbachias, you can cut the old stem into 2-inch sections, lay them on a bed of sand or peatmoss, cover lightly with either, and keep moist until shoots emerge from the ends of the cuttings and the bottom sides of the sections have developed roots. The many new plants can then be separately potted—and probably widely distributed to friends.

Root cuttings

Lift a complete plant from its pot or from the ground—but only when the plant is dormant—and cut sections of the larger, more fleshy roots into 2- to 3-inch-long pieces. Cut the end of the root nearest the crown of the plant (that would be the top of the root) straight across, and cut the other end on a slant, so you can distinguish top from bottom and won't plant the cuttings upside down. Insert the root cuttings in pots or flats of rooting medium with the straight cut at the surface level of the medium. The cuttings will develop roots, and growing points or crowns will form at the top ends of the cuttings.

Plant division

By pulling or cutting apart a large plant that has numerous shoots or buds growing together, any number of rooted sections can be obtained for separate potting. This is by far the quickest and easiest method of propagation. A large multiple-crowned African-violet readily produces a dozen or more new plants this way. Heleniums and chrysanthemums can be increased by the same means. Plants that grow from a single stem or crown cannot be propagated this way, of course.

Clumps of dahlia tubers can be cut into sizable divisions each with a bit of top growth; hardy bulbs, gladiolus and cyclamen corms can be cut in half. But wherever you have to use a knife, be sure it is sterile. Take care to dust all cut surfaces of a plant with sulfur or a fungicide like Fermate to prevent the entrance of disease.

Part Three

Plants to Grow
in Your Greenhouse

Greenhouse Plants

Here is a descriptive list of plants that you will enjoy growing in your greenhouse at one time or another during what I hope will be many years of greenhouse gardening for fun. Suggestions for culture are included, also names of many of the species and hybrids known to be most satisfactory for amateur gardeners who want results.

The list is in alphabetical order according to the botanical names of the plants. You're in very good company if, like many gardeners with a new greenhouse, you know a snapdragon when you see one but don't know that the botanical name is *Antirrhinum majus*. If you know a plant only by its popular or English name (shown in small capital letters in the list), look *that* name up in the Index, where you will be referred to the botanical name.

The temperature figures shown beside each plant indicate night temperature—useful information when you are deciding which plants you can grow in the night temperature at which you have decided to maintain your greenhouse (cool 45–50 F; moderate 55–60 F; or warm 65–70 F).

ABUTILON. FLOWERING-MAPLE. 45–55 F

Textured, intricately veined red, yellow, white, or pink flowers droop bell-like from slender stems; the leaves, which may be green or variegated, are shaped somewhat like those of a maple tree. Abutilons grow continuously, and sometimes become big and awkward, but this can

157

be controlled somewhat by keeping the plants potbound and giving supplemental fertilizer to make up for the restrictions of the roots, and by pinching growing tips of young plants. Give bright sun all year except part shade in summer; average soil; moderate watering. Usual flowering period is spring, summer, and fall, but they may flower the year around. Sow seed in spring for flowers in late fall. Take cuttings in spring and summer for mature plants in 4 to 6 months; fall cuttings take longer to mature. Recommended: *A Savitzii A. striatum Thompsonii* and the hybrids you will probably receive when you order from plant specialists. (See Color Plate III)

ACACIA.   40–50 F

Purchase one or two small greenhouse acacias from your local garden supplier, since cuttings usually take two years to reach satisfactory size. Acacias like a cool temperature and should be kept moist. Grow in sandy soil mixed with about one-third leafmold; give plenty of sunlight all year and free circulation of air. During March and April the misty green foliage forms a perfect background for drooping clusters of tiny yellow flowers. Allow plants to flower naturally; forcing results in bud-drop. After flowering, plants should be cut back and set out in the garden. Water frequently. In September, repot and return to the greenhouse for winter flowering. Pinch to induce branching and to inhibit excessive growth. Most acacias need really cool nights (about 40 F) during winter. Recommended: *A. decurrens dealbata, A. Baileyana, A. longifolia floribunda. Albizzia lophantha,* formerly known as *Acacia lophantha,* has tassel-like spikes of brilliant yellow flowers and takes the same culture recommended for acacias.

ACALYPHA.   55–65 F

Showy tropical shrubs with heart-shaped leaves and plushy flowers in long slender drooping tails. Plants are evergreen; flowering period is October to April. Full sun fall and winter, shade spring and summer; 60 per cent humidity preferred; grow in peatmoss, peatmoss and loam, or equal parts loam, peatmoss and sand; plants wilt easily so keep soil evenly moist in spring and summer, water moderately during fall and winter. Plants under 18 months of age do better at the 65 F night temperature, but mature plants get along nicely at 55 F. Propagate by 4-inch cuttings taken from almost-mature growth at any time of year, in sand or vermiculite in an enclosed case with 70 to 75 F bottom heat until cuttings are rooted. Recommended: *A. hispida,* REDHOT-CATTAIL, CHINILLE-PLANT, green leaves, bright red or purple flowers (see Color Plate IV); *A. hispida alba,* green leaves and creamy pinkish-white flowers; *A. Wilkesiana Macafeana,* COPPER-LEAF, bronzy green leaves marked with crimson and bronze, reddish flowers not especially attractive.

ACANTHUS mollis. BEAR'S-BREECH, ARCHITECTURAL-PLANT.   50–60 F

A compact, attractive, foliage plant that occasionally produces from the top of the plant a four-sided spike of whitish flowers. Gets along with 1 hour of sunlight a day; should have a short semi-dry rest in shade after flowering. Use an all-purpose mix kept moist during active growth. Propagate by seeds or division of the rhizome.

ACHIMENES. MAGIC-FLOWER.   60–65 F

If you have a spot in the greenhouse that will maintain a 60 F night temperature, try a few of these unusual-looking rhizomes, scaly enough to be mistaken for elongated pine cones. They are so prolific that even a single separated scale will produce a new plant. They are also propagated in spring by stem cuttings planted in damp sphagnum moss. The rhizomes may be planted any time from February to May in damp sphagnum moss or vermiculite. As soon as plants are large enough to handle, transfer to pots containing a soil mixture of equal parts sand, garden loam, and peatmoss or leafmold. Several plants to a bulb-pan make an interesting display, and the trailing species and hybrids are magnificent basket plants. Achimenes like a little sun in spring, bright shade in summer, and benefit from twice-monthly feedings. When blooming shows signs of tapering off, usually in October, hold back on the water and allow plants to finish their growing cycle. When growth ceases, remove the rhizomes (you will find they have multiplied prodigiously) from the pots or baskets, clean them off, and store in dry sand or vermiculite in a temperature of about 50 F until spring, when they can again be potted. Flowers will appear all summer in shades of pink, red, orange, white, and shades of blue to purple, if plantings are staggered. Warning: regardless of their stage of growth, achimenes will go into dormancy if the planting medium dries out just once, so keep the soil evenly moist but well drained.

AESCHYNANTHUS. LIPSTICK-PLANT.   **55–65 F**

A fibrous-rooted epiphytic evergreen trailing plant with waxy leaves, aeschynanthus flowers off and on throughout the year when given the culture suggested for gesneriads (page 219). Recommended: A. *Lobbianus* and A. *pulcher*, red flowers; A. *speciosa*, 4-inch-long orange and red flowers. (*Aeschynanthus* was formerly called *Trichosporum*, and some dealers still list it under the old name.)

AGAPANTHUS africanus. LILY-OF-THE-NILE.   **45–55 F**

The tender tuberous roots of this plant with fragrant blue lily-like bells above ribbon-like foliage (it attains a height of 3 feet) should be planted in March in rich soil consisting of equal parts of garden loam, peatmoss or leafmold, and well-rotted manure. Agapanthus likes plenty of moisture while growing during spring and while blooming through the summer, but taper off with the water during fall. While plants are dormant during winter, water sufficient only to prevent foliage from drying up should be given. Flowers (see Figure 48) of lovely shades of blue are produced all summer on long stems above fairly short, strap-like foliage. Twenty or more individual blossoms centrally joined to the tip of the long stem form a cluster of thin tube-like throats ending in six petals of lily-like florets. Agapanthus do best in tubs or large pots, as roots are strong and large; if sufficient root space is provided they will not have to be repotted for several years. Occasional applications of manure "tea" are helpful. Repotting, when necessary, should be done in late winter or very early spring before new growth starts. New plants may be started from root divisions at time of repotting. 'Peter Pan' is an 18-inch-tall dwarf variety with sky-blue flowers.

AGERATUM Houstonianum. FLOSS-FLOWER.   **45–50 F**

This long-time favorite of the outdoor garden is also excellent in the greenhouse. The habit of low growth and small leaves interspersed with candlewick tufts of white, blue, lavender, or pink make it ideal for pots or for planting along benches to make an attractive edging. Ageratum is nice for small flower arrangements and the lavender kinds are particularly attractive with yellow marigolds or pink zinnias. Provide a growing medium of equal thirds of soil, sand, and sphagnum moss, or use one of the pasteurized mixtures available at garden centers. Start seeds in February or March for greenhouse color or for setting out in the garden in spring. Sow in a flat and transplant to pots or bench after first true leaves (the second set) appear; or sow several seeds directly in a peat pot and thin out to one or two strong seedlings. Pinch out centers to induce branching. Repeat pinching several times to get full bushy plants. Recommended: 'Fairy Pink', 5 inches, salmon to rose-pink; 'Snow Carpet', 4 inches, uniform growth, pure white flowers. *Lonas inodora* is similar to ageratum in growth, flowers, and culture, and is sometimes called golden-ageratum.

AGLOANEMA simplex. CHINESE-EVERGREEN.   60–65 F

A foliage plant that needs very little light to exist but in the greenhouse it flowers. Flowers are not much to see, but the clusters of bright red berries that follow the flowers remain in good condition on the plant for two to three years. Grow in an all-purpose medium kept very moist (plant even grows in water). Propagate by stem cuttings.

48. *Agapanthus africanus.* (MERRY GARDENS PHOTO)

ALBUCA.   **45–50 F**

Fragrant blooms appear in spring and early summer from these tender bulbs that are dormant in summer. Full sun and fertile, porous soil are needed. Pot in early fall, keeping upper half of bulb above the soil; repotting will be needed only once in several years. Water freely and fertilize regularly from fall through spring; withhold water during summer dormancy. When foliage has ripened completely, store pots dry under a bench until the next season. Seed may be sown in spring or offsets may be taken from old bulbs when repotting. Recommended: *A. fastigiata,* white flower petals with green or brown tips; *A. major,* yellow flowers with a green stripe on each petal; *A. minor,* white flowers with center stripe of brick-red on each petal.

ALLAMANDA.   **60–70 F**

An evergreen climber with whorled waxy leaves, but it can be handled as a pot plant of convenient size if it is pruned. Grow in an all-purpose medium kept moist and fed twice monthly from April to September. Flowers appear from June to September; after flowering, keep plant almost dry from October to March. Prune to the desired size early in February. Propagate by cuttings with at least two joints anytime February to April; root in sand or vermiculite at 75–80 F, humid and shaded. Recommended: *A. cathartica* and *A. nerifolia,* golden-yellow funnel-shaped flowers; *A. violacea,* reddish-purple flowers.

ALLOPHYTON mexicanum. MEXICAN-FOXGLOVE.   **55–60 F**

A small perennial plant with crowded leaves on short stems, many half-inch-long lavender flowers to a cluster and numerous clusters to a plant almost continuously during the year. Full sun except some shading in summer; all-purpose medium kept moist. Propagate by seeds, which set readily; or divide plants.

ALOCASIA.   **65–70 F**

The ornamental arrow- or heart-shaped leaves, often variegated, may interest you in these foliage plants because the foliage colorings and patterns are so pretty. The leaves, however, are not less than a foot long and sometimes as wide, and you may not have space for a plant with flowers of little merit. Night temperature must never fall below 60 F and humidity must be high or plants drop their leaves. Plants need an abundance of water, porous soil with excellent drainage, and protection from direct sunlight. Progagation is by suckers (which alocasias produce readily) or by root cuttings. Try these two, both from Malaya: *A. cuprea,* leaves 1½ feet long and 1 foot across, purple on the underside and dark metallic shining green on top; *A. Korthalsii,* leaves about 14 inches long and 6 inches wide, white-veined olive-green on top and purple beneath.

ALSOPHILA australis. TREEFERN. 60–65 F

Really a tree, with a very straight heavy trunk and a beautifully proportioned spreading crown of light green, fluffy fronds. Needs filtered sunlight, grows slowly to 3 to 4 feet tall after several years, by which time it will need an 8- or 10-inch pot. Meticulous attention to watering is required, because this treefern, delightful for accent in a greenhouse full of flowers, does not survive a drying out. Will do well only in a greenhouse that maintains high humidity and 60 F at night.

ALSTROEMERIA. PERUVIAN-LILY. 50–60 F

The tender fleshy roots are potted in autumn in large pots or garden loam and well-rotted manure. Give plenty of water while plants are growing. Funnel-shaped blossoms about 1½ inches long branch from a single stem, appear for several months usually starting in March. When blooming is finished, plants will go completely dormant and roots should be removed from the pot and stored in a dry, cool place until time for repotting. Propagate by root division before repotting in spring, or by seeds planted in August. Recommended: *A. Pelegrina,* lilac flowers spotted with red-purple; *A. Pelegrina alba,* white flowers.

ALTERNANTHERA amoena. JOSEPH'S-COAT. 60–65 F

Small, branching bushy plants with leaves of many colors, resembling a twisted coleus; small white flowers most of the time. All-purpose medium kept moist (plants wilt easily). Shear the plants occasionally to keep them compact. Propagate by stem cuttings or root division.

✕AMARCRINUM. 55–65 F

Handsome, exquisitely fragrant flowers from tender bulbs that should be potted with half the bulb above the surface of the soil, and repotted every three to four years in March, in sandy, acid soil. Amarcrinums are evergreen, but they may be dried off and the bulbs stored in pots (like amaryllis) if you can't spare the space for them when they are not in bloom. Flowering time is winter and early spring. As ×*Amarcrinum* is a hybrid between *Amaryllis* and *Crinum,* many beautiful varieties are available.

AMOMUM Cardamon. SPICY GINGER-PLANT.   60–65 F

A very large foliage plant worth the space it takes if you are fond of a spicy aroma. The dark green bamboo-like foliage emits the scent when crushed or rubbed. Rich soil, protection from strong sun, and abundant moisture are needed. Sometimes these plants appear to have stopped growing—in this semi-dormant stage, don't dry them out completely, but water sparingly until activity is again apparent.

ANEMONE coronaria. WINDFLOWER.   45–50 F

Here is a brilliant, colorful, poppy-like flower ideal for the cool greenhouse. A night temperature of no more than 45–50 F is necessary to assure blooming, and they can be grown from corms potted in September or seed sown in late spring. If you start from corms, use a mixture of rich loam, peatmoss and sand. Place a layer of broken crock or gravel in the bottom of a bulb-pan, fill with soil to about 2 inches from the top. Press the pointed end of the corm into the mixture about 1 inch and space corms 2 to 3 inches apart, depending on the size of the bulb-pan. Cover with another inch of soil and a quarter-inch of clean, sharp sand, vermiculite or other sterile medium to help prevent damp-off. Water sparingly until top growth is evident and keep cool; brilliant flowers of white, red, or blue-purple appear from January through March. When flowering has diminished, remove corms from pots and dry out for storing in a cool place until the following September. Anemones may be grown from seed sown in sphagnum moss or other sterile medium to prevent damp-off. When large enough to handle, transfer the young plants to a large bulb-pan, where they will furnish blooms all winter starting in October.

ANTHURIUM. FLAMINGO-FLOWER.   65–70 F

Small to very large plants that are almost everblooming if the new roots along the aerial stems are kept covered with damp sphagnum moss. Use an all-purpose soil mix, or one for epiphytic plants, and keep it wet. Tropical conditions of warmth, high humidity, and bright light but no direct sunlight promote "flowers" (actually spathes) in all shades of red, pink, orange. Propagate by suckers, root cuttings, or seeds. Recommended: *A. Andraeanum, A. Scherzerianum.*

ANTIRRHINUM majus. SNAPDRAGON. 45–55 F

One of my favorites for easy growing and an endless supply of cut flowers of clear or blended shades of yellow, rose, red pink, lavender, orange, bronze, and white. (See Color Plate I and Figure 27.) Sown on sphagnum in standard flats or composition peat flats for a winter crop, F_1 hybrid seeds (developed specially for greenhouse growing) germinate in 7 to 10 days. Sprinkle seed over peat or moss that has been soaked and squeezed free of excess water. Insert the flat in a plastic bag and seal to retain moisture and provide warmth for germination. At first sign of growth, remove the plastic. When true leaves appear and seedlings are big enough to handle, transplant to bench in rows 3 inches apart. To provide adequate air circulation, I stagger the rows so plants are not opposite, and each has more than 3 inches of growing space. Snapdragons require little or no fertilizing until plants are established. Tall kinds require support. If you plan to grow them regularly for several years, install bench wiring frames; otherwise, makeshift wiring will be satisfactory and less expensive. I nail thin green cane stakes to the bench and tie the plant up with green string. Snapdragons may be grown to single stems, or they may be pinched; I prefer growing to single stems. After these are cut, side shoots bloom, but not so straight or full-blown as the first cuttings. Still, they provide nice flowers for a long time. Snapdragons to be pinched should be spaced about 8 inches apart in the bench. After seedlings are established, pinch to leave three pairs of leaves. Discard plants when flowering has stopped. Snapdragons can be grown the year around, so check types and flowering dates when you purchase seeds. Keep in mind that germination is more rapid in summer. Recommended: 'Floral Carpetrose', the first dwarf F_1 hybrid snapdragons; 'Hit Parade', a mixture of creamy white, bright yellow, pink lavender, and bright red F_1 hybrids.

APHELANDRA squarrosa Louisae. ZEBRA-PLANT. 55–65 F

Yellow flowers on square terminal spikes, white-veined shiny green foliage. After flowering from September to November, keep the plant growing until about March, then take 4-inch tip cuttings for new plants rather than trying to make the old one repeat a second year. Grow in an all-purpose mix, keeping it evenly moist as aphelandras wilt easily. Give some sun in winter, partial shade during summer.

ARAUCARIA excelsa. NORFOLK-ISLAND-PINE.   50–60 F

A permanent plant that requires practically no attention, looks like a little live Christmas tree self-decorated with its own light-green growing tips, and grows 6 to 8 inches a year. An all-purpose mix is satisfactory, if you allow the plant to get almost dry between waterings. Propagate by rooting the top of an old plant. Side branches will root but they do not form a nicely shaped tree.

ARDISIA crispa. CORAL-BERRY.   55–65 F

Add color to your house at Christmas time with several pots of this compact shrub (formerly called *Ardisia crenulata*) with drooping coral-red flowers that become bright red berries. Give plenty of light, but shade lightly from bright sun during summer. Grow at 65 F; after berries set about October first, temperature may be lowered to 55 F. Equal parts garden loam, peatmoss, and sand with a small amount of well-rotted manure added seems to be the best potting mixture. Ardisias may be reproduced from seed, but cuttings produce best. Remove a strip of bark directly below the foliage, clear around the stem; wrap wet moss around the cut area, keep moist, and a good root system will develop in 6 to 8 weeks, at which time the new plant can be cut from the shrub and potted in the mixture mentioned above. Cuttings should be taken in late spring.

AUCUBA japonica variegata. GOLD-DUST-TREE.   40–45 F

Although this plant is classified as a cool greenhouse plant, it tolerates great extremes of temperature from hot to cold. The glossy leaves appear to be sprinkled with gold-dust. Aucuba likes plenty of fresh air and good light, but has been known to do well where light is very poor. A mixture of garden loam, decayed manure, and peatmoss is good for growing. Some sand may be added to provide good drainage, since it likes to be grown dry and should be allowed to become moderately dry between waterings.

AZALEA.   45–65 F

For a brilliant display of colorful single or double blossoms, it pays to purchase plants from specialists for growing on to maturity. If blossoms are desired during the Christmas season, select plants with buds already well set. Plants usually come burlapped; put the wrapped root-ball in a bucket of water, soak thoroughly and then drain well. Azaleas are acid-loving plants and do exceptionally well when planted in peat-moss in small pots, as roots like to be closely contained. Keep well moistened, but do not saturate. A fine misting or syringing daily encourages bud development. Temperature of 60 F starting late in September should force buds to open by Christmas; bud development can be held back by dropping temperature to 45 F. Store pots in a cool garage or cellar and bring a few at a time into the greenhouse for forc-ing into a continuing period of bloom, much the same as you schedule spring bulbs. Provide some shade from extremely bright sun and give plenty of fresh air. To carry plants over the summer, set them out in the garden in spring, after danger of frost is over; plunge pots to the rim or plant directly in soil in a damp cool area. Water frequently. Sunshine from August on will promote bud development. Lift from garden in September, repot in fresh peatmoss in a pot just slightly larger than the rootball. If plants are kept in pots all summer, they will usually go two years without repotting, and should be transferred to the new pot im-mediately after flowering has ceased in spring. Azaleas are propagated from cuttings taken in May; bottom heat of 65 F is required, and cut-tings should be protected from direct sun and misted frequently. Use a mixture of peatmoss and clean sharp sand. After about 5 weeks roots will be developed sufficiently to move plants to flats of peatmoss; keep evenly moist. Shift to a second flat for further development and then to pots. Pinch to induce branching. Loss of foliage indicates insufficient moisture or poor light. Yellowing of leaves can be corrected by water-ing with ½ ounce of iron sulphate dissolved in 1 gallon of water. Rec-ommended: 'Alaska', semi-double white, early blooming; 'Coral Bells', light pink, early blooming; 'Hahn's Red', single fringed red, midseason bloom; 'Jean Haerens', bright pink double, late blooming; 'Veraeneana Rosea', double oranged-red, midseason bloom.

BEGONIAS.

You will probably find, after gardening in your greenhouse for six months to a year, that begonias impress you as being among the most reliable and colorful plants you have. Careful selection from among the thousands of kinds available will keep you in flowers all year, in every color except blue (see Figures 22, 36, 40, 49–54). From the standpoint of culture, it is best to handle begonias according to their root or stem structure, rather than by foliage and flower forms.

Summer-flowering tuberous begonias   60–65 F

For a truly beautiful display of flowers, try some of these. Hybrids are brilliantly handsome in color and form, and produce large flowers sometimes 8 to 10 inches across when properly cultivated. Colors include white, yellow, apricot through pink, salmon to red, and picotee forms. Flowers may be single, double, crested, ruffled, frilled; flower forms resemble carnations, roses, rosebuds, and camellias.

Start tubers in March in a mixture of leafmold and sand or in milled sphagnum moss, as soon as tiny pink shoots appear in the indentation in the tuber. Settle tuber into mixture until entire tuber is covered and shoots are just at the surface of the soil. When roots are well established, transplant to pots in a light, fibrous, well-drained soil mixture. (Summer-flowering tuberous begonias are one- sided plants, that is, the flowers always face in the direction in which the leaves point.) Water well and place in a section of the greenhouse where plants will get filtered sunlight. Bright sun burns blossoms; too much shade makes the plants leggy. Take care not to allow water to collect in the concave top of the tuber from which the stems grow; this often causes tubers to rot.

If, after blooming for a while during the summer, your tuberous begonias seem suddenly to go into a decline, keep them on the dry side for about three weeks. This will induce new growth. Fertilize to strengthen this new growth and remove old stems. The new blooming period will carry through till autumn. This summer hiatus in blooming can be avoided if you remove the first few flower buds produced by the plant, giving it a chance to build a sufficiently strong root system to sustain it during the exhausting flowering period. The first flowers are usually small and of poor quality, anyway, so unless you just can't wait to see the flowers, do remove the first buds to allow the plant to build into a specimen able to support the large flowers.

When plants start dying off in the fall, withhold water and let the pots dry out completely. Remove all roots and dead foliage and store tubers in dry sphagnum moss or dry sand at a temperature of 40 to 50 F until new growth is evident. Then the growing procedure may be started again.

Tuberous begonias may be started from seed in February for summer or fall flowering. The extremely fine seed should be broadcast on dampened milled sphagnum moss, preferably in a seed flat. Cover with glass but nothing else—light is essential to germination, as is a night temperature of 65 to 70 F. At no time during germination must the medium dry out, hence the use of sterile sphagnum moss to prevent damp-off from too much moisture. When seedlings are large enough to handle, pot them in a mixture of leafmold, garden loam, and well-rotted manure, and treat the same as newly started tubers.

Recommended: 'A. L. Berry', double yellow; 'Ballerina', a group of double-ruffled hybrids in pink, yellow, apricot; 'Red Triumph', ruffled frilled ruby red; 'Santa Maria', ruffled pure white; 'Charmain', double pink; 'Flambeau', double orange-scarlet; 'Mandarin', double salmon-orange; 'Stars and Stripes', rose-colored camellia-type flowers blotched with white.

Pendent tuberous begonias   60–65 F

Wonderful for baskets, these are available in several colors and in single or double flowers. Start tubers in January, following procedure recommended above for summer-flowering tuberous begonias. In about four weeks they will be ready to transplant to a basket, three or four evenly spaced (depending on size of basket), in a mixture of three parts leafmold, one part well-rotted manure, and one part sharp sand. They should be in flower by June if fertilized once a month and kept in filtered sunlight. Dry off and store tubers in fall, same as the other summer-flowering tuberous begonias.

Winter-flowering tuberous begonias   55–60 F

There are two types of these small-scale replicas of summer-flowering tuberous begonias: hiemalis, the larger and more lavishly blooming; and cheimantha ("Christmas begonia") with smaller single flowers in white or shades of pink. Both types flower in winter but do not necessarily go completely dormant in summer.

Cheimanthas bloom from November to March in draft-free, humid but fresh air, soil constantly moist but not soggy; plenty of bright light but not much direct sun. When flowering stops, cut plants back severely, continue to keep cool and moist until new shoots appear. When these have two or more nodes, cut them off and root them in a propagating box for the next year's plants. Recommended: 'Carolina', 'Marina',

'Spirit of Norway', 'Gloire de Lorraine', 'Marjorie Gibbs', and 'Lady Mac' which is often listed as "Christmas White" or "Christmas Pink" begonia.

Hiemalis begonias, with showy double flowers or dogwood-like single flowers up to 4 inches across in white and shades of pink, red, salmon, and apricot, are more susceptible to mildew and rot than the cheimanthas, but the plants can be saved from year to year. Recommended: 'Apricot Beauty', 'Emily Clibran', 'Baardse's Wonder', 'Fairy', 'Pink Perfection', 'Snowdrop', 'The President'.

Rhizomatous begonias   60–70 F

Most of the beautifully foliaged Rex begonias are rhizomatous, that is, they have a thick stem or rhizome from which the leaves, flowers, and roots grow. The rhizome creeps on top of the soil, not through it.

49. White Christmas begonia. (MERRY GARDENS PHOTO)

50. Begonia 'Maphil'. (MERRY GARDENS PHOTO)

51. Begonia 'Skeezar'. (MERRY GARDENS PHOTO)

52. *Begonia Sunderbruchii.* (MERRY GARDENS PHOTO)

These begonias have extremely shallow roots and do best in azalea-type pots. No direct sun for these—it fades the stunning foliage colors. Usually, rhizomatous begonias stop growing during winter's short days; a few even lose their foliage and appear to be dead. They all become active again in early spring.

Fibrous-rooted begonias   55–70 F

Everyone knows the old-fashioned, dependable *Begonia semperflorens,* called everblooming or wax begonias. They are easy to grow in a mixture of three parts soil and one part peatmoss. Seeds sown in June will produce 3-inch blooming plants by Christmas; stem cuttings can be taken any time and rooted quickly in water, then potted in 2-inch pots. Plants should be pinched to keep them compact and bushy so more flowering shoots will develop. Feeding about every three weeks encourages steady flowering. Recommended: 'Carol', 'Cinderella Red', 'Pink Camellia', 'South Pacific', 'Spun Rose', 'Thimbleberry'; also the so-called "calla-lily" wax begonias, as 'Charm'.

Cane-stemmed or *angelwing* begonias are often big and sprawly, and these are best grown in a basket or suspended pot. They are unusually sensitive to a direct draft, which can cause immediate dropping of foliage from all along the stem. If this happens, cut the stem off close to the pot and new sprouts will soon appear. Recommended: 'Dainty Spray', 'May Queen', 'Orange Rubra', 'Pinafore'.

There are many *small-leaved branching begonias* with delightful foliage and rarely without flowers. Good in baskets are 'Shippy's Garland' and 'Mme. Fanny Giron'; and for either baskets or pots try 'Catalina', 'Digswelliana', 'It', and especially 'Preussen'.

The *hirsute* (hairy) *begonias* require less humidity than the others,

53. White-flowered "calla-lily" begonia.

(MERRY GARDENS PHOTO)

54. Begonia 'It'.

(MERRY GARDENS PHOTO)

and will not tolerate overwatering. Try 'Alleryi', 'Mrs. Fred D. Scripps', *B. metallica, B. Scharffiana,* 'Lady Clare', 'Richland', and especially 'San Miguel'.

BELOPERONE guttata. SHRIMP-PLANT.   50–55 F

An excellent pot plant for year-round "flowers" that are really showy bracts. Needs plenty of fresh air and bright sun. Soak thoroughly, then dry out somewhat before watering again. Pot in a mixture of one-third each garden loam, well-rotted manure, and humus or peat. Prune frequently; root the tip cuttings, which will bloom the first year.

BOUGAINVILLEA glabra.   60–65 F

If not controlled, this vine would crowd everything else out of the greenhouse, but it adapts very well to being grown as a pot plant when it is cut back to under 12 inches every spring. Bougainvilleas flower from early fall to late spring (there are some hybrids that flower the year around) with colorful bracts of white, salmon, purple-red, and yellow. Equal-thirds soil mix, full sun, twice-monthly feeding, evenly moist. Propagate by 3-inch tip cuttings, which will be flowering plants within a year.

BOUVARDIA.   55–65 F

A handsome evergreen shrub with clusters of white, pink, or red flowers. The white bouvardias have a sweet jasmine-like scent. Purchase your first plant and make cuttings if you desire to grow more than one. Take stem cuttings in spring and root in a mixture of clean sharp sand and peat over bottom heat. Transfer to 2½-inch pots—two or three cuttings to a pot—containing soil with an abundance of leafmold or other organic matter, on the alkaline side. Never allow bouvardias to want for water. Apply weak solutions of high-nitrogen fertilizer. Give full sun except during the peak heat of summer, when light shading is necessary to prevent scorching of foliage. Stagger pinching while plant is in active growth to promote flowering from June to January. Plants should be cut back after flowering and given less water until February. If plants are shaded with black cloth for a month after flowering ceases, and grown at 65 F or higher, they may be brought into flower a second time. Recommended: *B. ternifolia,* red flowers; *B. Humboldtii,* fragrant white flowers.

55. *Tillandsia ionantha,* a bromeliad. (MERRY GARDENS PHOTO)

BROMELIADS.   60–70 F

Bromeliads are a strange but fascinating group, mostly air plants (epiphytes) that adapt readily to pot culture in a mix of equal parts garden loam, peatmoss, leafmold, and sand; or in coarse sphagnum moss alone. They seem to be immune to pests, easy to grow, indestructible, available in many sizes from miniature to very large; the foliage is highly colored, the flowers exotic in color and structure, and some species have berries that last three to four months. Provide shade and high humidity, and water by filling the "vase" in the center of the rosette of leaves. Let a little water spill over to the medium, but always keep the vases filled. Most bromeliads flower once, then eventually die; but you can perpetuate them by removing the offsets from the base of parent plant (offsets usually appear after plant has flowered) and rooting them in moist vermiculite at 75 to 85 F, high humidity, and shade. Recommended: species and hybrids of *Aechmea, Ananas, Billbergia, Cryptanthus, Dyckia, Greigia, Gusmania, Neoregelia, Tillandsia* (Figure 55), and *Vriesia.*

56. *Browallia speciosa alba.* (MERRY GARDENS PHOTO)

BROWALLIA speciosa. 50–60 F

Emerald-green foliage and lavender-blue or snowy-white flowers make lovely plantings for a hanging basket; add an ivy-leaved geranium like pink-flowered 'Santa Paula' and you will be delighted with the effect. Browallias are also excellent pot plants, several to a 5- or 6-inch bulb-pan. For best flowering, grow near the heater as these thrive with more warmth than most other plants in the cool greenhouse. Sow seed in February for spring bloom, in July and August for winter flowers; seeds germinate in 15 days. Grow in sun or partial shade. Pinch plants repeatedly to induce branching and to show off the flower clusters to advantage. Recommended: *B. speciosa alba* (Figure 56); 'Blue Bells', lavender-blue flowers; 'Silver Bells', glistening white flowers.

BRUNSFELSIA. KISS-ME-QUICK. 50–55 F

Very fragrant flowers, usually lavender-blue aging to white within a day or two but remaining on the plant and giving it the appearance of having several colors of flowers at the same time; blooms from January into summer, needs rich soil, regular feeding, and does best when kept potbound. Fragrance is strongest at night. Give filtered or diffused sunlight, keep soil evenly moist. Propagate by cuttings from new growth in spring. Recommended: *B. americana, B. calycina, B. latifolia.*

CACTI and SUCCULENTS. 60–70 F

If you are a plant enthusiast with a consuming interest in nature's unusual and dramatic manifestations, surely the category of cacti and other succulent plants intrigues you. Nowhere else in the plant world will you find a more fascinating array of weird and unusual forms, or more exotically colorful blossoms. Furthermore, few other plants are so rewarding in return for so little attention.

These plants are native to desert and to jungle, where they are subjected to long periods of extreme heat and drought, and they have accommodated themselves to their environments by producing very small leaves and coverings of fleshy stems, spines, or scales to reduce evaporation of stored moisture so essential to life during dry spells. Many cacti and succulents are small enough, and stay that way, to be ideal for the greenhouse growers interested in collecting many kinds. As to the distinction between them: all cacti are succulents, but all succulents are not cacti.

Despite cold desert nights, cacti and succulents grow best in a greenhouse of at least 60 F at night. Soil mixtures vary slightly, depending upon the origin of the plants. Those from the desert thrive in an equal-thirds mixture of peatmoss, sand, and garden loam; those from jungle areas should have an equal part of leafmold added to the desert mix. Desert cacti take full sun all year, but they do not suffer if given the light shading required by the jungle types. Desert cacti, inured to extreme heat, burning sun, and only occasional periods of heavy rain, are

57. *Opuntia compressa,* prickly-pear cactus. (ROCHE PHOTO)

grown on the dry side. Jungle types are better kept evenly moist since the dense growth and high humidity of the tropics tends to maintain moisture. An occasional period of drying out is apparently beneficial, but put plants on a twice-a-month feeding schedule starting in February when growth begins after the winter rest and continuing into September. In winter give little water while plants are in an almost dormant period.

Each species or variety of cactus has its own blooming season. If you grow cacti primarily for flowers, special handling is necessary. Plants must rest for three months prior to their flowering time at a daytime temperature no higher than 60 F; give plenty of light but hold back on the water. At the first indication of new growth, resume your schedule of watering and feeding and provide normal temperatures. Repot plants when it is evident they are rootbound; do this between February and June, though September is also satisfactory. At other seasons, dis-

58. *Crassula multicava,* a low-growing succulent with oval leaves and white to pale pink flowers. (MERRY GARDENS PHOTO)

turb the roots as little as possible. Small plants should be repotted to the next larger pot each year; repot mature plants every three years.

Several methods of propagation can be used to increase your collection: cuttings, root divisions, offsets, grafts, or seeds.

Seed germination takes only about 10 to 20 days. Damp-off is the biggest problem to overcome. Use a sterilized medium. Water thoroughly, cover with glass, and shade with newspaper until germination, then remove the coverings. When spines appear on seedlings, transplant to flats containing a soil mixture as recommended above for mature plants, screened to remove lumps and large particles. Withhold water for several days after transplanting, then water regularly.

Make cuttings with a clean, sharp knife. If the plant has branches, cut off a branch from the main section; if it grows to a single stem, take a 2- to 3-inch cutting from the upper part of the stem, usually during spring or summer. To avoid stem rot, place cutting in a shady, dry location and let the cut heal until the base looks thickened—this takes from a week to a month. When cut is well healed, insert in sand or sterile medium such as perlite, and water sparingly for a few days, giving only enough moisture to prevent shriveling. When cuttings have rooted, move to small pots.

To propagate by offsets, separate them gently from the main plant and pot individually in regular planting mix.

Try grafting to produce novel and unusual cacti. The operation is simple and almost always successful. Two or more types can be grafted together, and almost all kinds are compatible. Slice each specimen horizontally to provide the flat cut surfaces which are fastened tightly together. Use rubber bands or string over the top and under the pot and crossed at right angles, to assure close contact until the graft "takes." Or make a V-shaped cut in the potted plant, and shape the bottom of the piece to be grafted to fit into the V. Tie together and do not disturb until healed.

Cleanliness is extremely important in growing cacti and succulents. Insect infestations are troublesome, and the plants will not tolerate some of the newer pesticides such as parathion or malathion. Mealybugs, scale, spider-mites, thrips, and aphids may be controlled with rotenone, pyrethrum, or nicotine preparations. Prevent nematodes and damp-off by steam sterilizing soil before use. Once infested with nematodes, plant must be destroyed.

There are thousands of cacti and other succulents suitable for growing in a greenhouse, so you should obtain catalogues from specialists and use the detailed descriptions and illustrations to help you select what you would like to grow. I can recommend the species and hybrids of these genera:

Cacti: *Aporophyllum* (Color Plate III), *Astrophytum, Cephalocereus, Cleistocactus, Echinocactus, Echinocereus, Echinopsis, Gymnocalycium, Hylocereus, Lemaireocereus, Lobivia* (Color Plate IV), *Mammillaria, Notocactus, Opuntia* (Figure 57), *Parodia, Rebutia, Rhipsalidopsis* (Color Plate IV), *Selenicereus.*

Succulents: *Adromischus, Aeonium, Aichryson, Cotyledon, Crassula* (Color Plate III, and Figure 58), *Echeveria, Faucaria, Fenestraria, Gasteria, Graptopetalum, Haworthia, Hereroa, Kalanchoe, Kleinia, Ophthalmophyllum* (Color Plate III), *Oscularia, Othonna, Pachyphytum, Portulacaria,* and *Sedum.*

CALADIUM.   60–70 F

The variegated leaves of this delightful foliage plant range from long, slender lance-like tips of the new dwarf varieties to the immensely large elephant-ear specimens. The familiar transparently thin, white-leaved kinds intricately veined with green resemble huge arrowheads. Caladium foliage comes in shades of crimson, rose, scarlet, yellow, and green; spotted, veined, or margined in darker hues or contrasting colors. Tubers or rhizomes are started in spring in sphagnum moss in a warm 75 to 85 F temperature. They require very little water until well started. When plants are established, shift them to pots, using a soil mixture of equal parts leafmold, sand, and horticultural charcoal. Once potted, they like plenty of water, so provide good drainage to prevent sogginess. Caladiums can stand sun or partial shade, and benefit from a weekly feeding of liquid manure. Foliage dies back in the fall and tubers may be stored in the pots placed on their sides under the bench. Or, remove tubers from pot and store in sand or dry peatmoss until spring. You can grow caladiums without worrying about insects or disease. Recommended: 'Fannie Munson', clear, luminous pink leaves with narrow green border; 'Mrs. F. M. Joyner', white leaves with scarlet ribs when shaded, but copper red in partial sun; 'White Christmas', symmetrical pattern of one-half of leaf area pure white, other half Christmas green; 'Candidum', snow white with green netting of veins.

CALCEOLARIA crenatiflora. LADY'S-POCKETBOOK.   **45–50 F**

The pouch-like flowers of this colorful pot plant never cease to be a conversation piece in any greenhouse. Shades of red, yellow, and bronze spotted with brown are available in double-pouch hybrids, or in dwarf 9-inch tall varieties. Seeds, which are extremely fine, should be broadcast on top of the planting medium, covered only with glass shaded with newspaper until germination. Transplant to 3-inch pots, then to 5's or 6's at flowering time. Careful watering is necessary at all times to prevent crown rot. Allow plenty of air circulation and shade from direct sunlight to prevent burning flowers. Usually no fertilizer is necessary until plants mature, then weekly applications of dilute fertilizer, or full-strength applications every 3 to 4 weeks. Plants from seed sown in August or September start to bloom in March if extra light is given from 5:00 to 10:00 p.m. starting the middle of December. Normal blooming time is May. Discard plants after flowering. Recommended: Duplex Hybrids, bushy, fairly dwarf plants with red, yellow, or bronze flowers; Dwarf Compact (Figure 59), 9-inches tall, easy to handle, flowers in clusters of reds, yellows, and intermediate shades, solid or spotted.

59. New Dwarf Compact Calceolaria. (GEORGE W. PARK SEED CO. PHOTO)

CALENDULA officinalis. POT MARIGOLD.   **45–50 F**

One of the showiest of greenhouse bench plants, with 4-inch or larger flowers of delicate creamy white through apricot to dark orange, produced over a 6-month period. Heat-resistant types bloom freely on long straight stems, furnishing long-lasting cut flowers well into summer. Sow seed (germination 10 days) toward end of July for January flowers, in October for February and March bloom, and in November for flowers through June. Mulch with peatmoss to prevent damp-off, and remove some of the lower leaves to allow free circulation of air and avoid stem rot. A soil mix containing well-rotted manure and superphosphate produces superior flowers. Set plants 10 to 12 inches apart in bench to give room for branching. Pinch out terminal bud to produce more flowers on new growth. For large exhibition blooms, remove all but one bud from each stem. Water plants freely and give plenty of sunshine. Discard plants when flowering season ends. Recommended: Art Shades, 2-feet tall plants with apricot, cream, orange, lemon flowers in mixture; 'Flame', 2-feet tall, clear brilliant orange heat-resistant flowers up to 5-inch across.

CAMELLIAS.   **40–50 F**

If you plan to devote your entire greenhouse to camellias, consider having rio benches. Most greenhouse camellias are of average size, and though they grow slowly eventually they attain a height impractical for benches. In a narrow greenhouse, you might find it more practical to place a bench on one side and none on the other. In this arrangement, plants will not all be at one height, but low on one side of the house and high on the other, making it easier to move through the center of the greenhouse. As I do not specialize exclusively in camellias, I removed a 5-foot section of bench on one side and placed my five potted camellias on the ground, keeping the rest of the house benched for my orchids. Camellias require very little care, and even when not in flower the glossy dark green foliage of this evergreen shrub is pleasing.

Camellias are said to prefer a temperature of 42 to 45 F, but I have had unbelievable results with mine grown at 52 F night temperature. A soil mix of two parts garden soil, one part peatmoss, and one part sand is recommended. Camellias like soil on the acid side, and good drainage is necessary. They like plenty of water; I soak mine thoroughly

60. Camellia. (GEORGE W. PARK SEED CO. PHOTO)

every other day all year round, and mist the foliage every other day in cool weather, every day during summer, until flower buds begin to swell. Then I spray a fine water mist into the air above the shrubs rather than directly onto the foliage.

Applications of iron chelate and a complete fertilizer such as Ra-Pid-Gro or fish oil emulsion (my favorite) alternated monthly during active growth are beneficial in conditioning the shrub to bloom prolifically. Iron chelate corrects iron deficiency in soil. It can be used as a foliage spray (1 level teaspoon per gallon of water), or applied to the soil according to size of shrub: 1 teaspoon for plants up to 2 feet, 2 teaspoons for plants 2 to 3 feet tall, and 1 tablespoon per plant for larger woody shrubs. Dissolve the iron chelate granules in a convenient volume of water and apply to the soil; or mix with a small amount of soil or sand sprinkled on top of soil and watered in thoroughly.

When growth activity increases in spring immediately after flowering ends, maintain humidity of at least 50 per cent. Misting the foliage, as mentioned previously, helps to raise the humidity, as does wetting down the walk and surrounding area.

Camellias require light shading. My roller-type shades are kept halfway down the roof in winter, midway between eave and ground in summer. In addition, vinyl plastic shading covers the gable glass in the south end of the greenhouse where my camellias grow. Camellias like a free circulation of air. They may be summered in the garden in semi-shade, as under a tree or in a lath-house. If your greenhouse is climate controlled like mine, they may be kept under glass all year.

To restrain the size of the shrub, prune slightly in spring just after flowering. If you prefer fewer but larger flowers, remove all but the main bud from the cluster at the end of each stem when buds are still small (about the size of a pea). However, if cultural directions are followed carefully, you will probably not have to disbud to get good-sized blooms, and your shrubs will be a riot of flowers and color if all buds are allowed to mature.

Plants purchased from a camellia specialist will probably be growing in large metal containers, and it will be unnecessary to shift them for several years. Mine are still in the containers they came in, and I haven't even added new topsoil; the blossoms this fifth year were so prolific you could hardly see the leaves. When repotting is necessary, take care of this task in spring right after flowering ceases and before new growth starts. Small plants will probably require repotting each year. Larger plants can be given an annual top dressing of fresh soil for several years before shifting into larger containers.

Camellias are reproduced by seed, cuttings, layering, or grafting. It takes from four to seven years to produce flowering plants from seed, but if you would like to try, sow seeds ½-inch deep in a mix of one part garden soil and one part peatmoss, with a little sand added for good drainage. Transplant to small pots when 6 inches tall. Cuttings are taken in fall from fresh growth, each at least 3 inches long. Place in sand in a propagating case with bottom heat of about 70 F; in two to three months cuttings will be rooted, ready to pot in 2½-inch pots. Shift to larger pots as necessary.

Camellias may be susceptible to scale, aphids, mealy bugs, and red-spider infestations, but as they are grown so cool and moist, little trouble will be encountered if good air circulation is maintained. Flower buds may drop if humidity is too low, if temperature fluctuates markedly, or if soil is allowed to dry out at any time.

You will do well to purchase mature plants from a local garden center or camellia specialist. Choose varieties with different flowering dates so you will have camellia flowers for six months of the year. The selection is wide: pink, red, white with red markings, rosy-pink; single, double, semi-double, and peony-type blossoms. Mine are all in clear pink shades: 'Flirtation' has 3½-inch single blossoms, 'Brigadoon' has 4½-inch crisp, firm, double flowers.

61. *Campanula isophylla alba.* (MERRY GARDENS PHOTO)

CAMPANULA isophylla. BELLFLOWER, FALLING-STAR.   **45–55 F**

An ideal hanging-basket or shelf plant with wide-open star-shaped blue or lavender-blue blossoms that cover the trailing stems during summer and fall. The white flowers of the very popular *C. isophylla alba* (Figure 61) are particularly attractive. Campanulas like lots of fresh air, and good light except during summer when they should be lightly shaded. Soil can be garden loam, or good garden soil with well-rotted manure and peat or humus added. Sow seed in spring in peat pots which are put in the basket when plants are large enough. Pinch frequently up to the end of May to insure bushy plants. Water well during summer but allow soil to become fairly dry between waterings. Apply a complete fertilizer while plants are in active growth. In late fall, when plants show signs of diminishing bloom, cut back to about 6 inches and continue in growth on the dry side. In spring when a new growing cycle begins, repot in fresh soil and increase watering. As soon as spring growth is established, cuttings can be taken to start new plants.

CARISSA grandiflora nana compacta. NATAL-PLUM.   **50–60 F**

Grow at least one of these compact small shrubs with glossy foliage. Showy white lily-scented blossoms are followed by red fruit. Ideal for greenhouse culture as it likes good light and plenty of fresh air; bright sun is not harmful. Use a loamy soil with well-rotted manure and peat or humus added in equal thirds. Keep evenly moist, insure good drainage, and mist the foliage frequently—high humidity is often the means of promoting bud formation. Water sparingly when plant is resting. Propagate by cuttings.

CEROPEGIA Woodii. ROSARY-VINE, HEART-VINE.   **50–55 F**

Very interesting and quite different from most vines; heart-shaped silver-spotted leaves of varying sizes and tiny waxy pink-purple flowers on a tangle of stringy vines. Ceropegia needs a temperature of 50 to 55 F so select its location carefully. Buy your first one and propagate by cuttings rooted in sand or by planting the little tubers that follow flowers on the vines. Pot rooted cuttings or sprouted tubers in soil rich in humus or leafmold; sand or perlite should be added for good drainage, and peatmoss is beneficial to root systems. Use a complete fertilizer. Grow in filtered or diffused sunlight; water thoroughly, then let become moderately dry before watering again. *C. Barklyi* (umbrella-plant) is also fascinating to grow.

62. *Chlorophytum comosum.* (MERRY GARDENS PHOTO)

CHLOROPHYTUM. SPIDER-PLANT. 50–55 F

Slender green-and-white-striped grasslike foliage sprays out and down from a center rosette. Fleshy runners in spring terminate in little plantlets bearing dainty white flowers. Garden loam to which well-rotted manure and peat have been added, plus a little sand for good drainage, makes a good potting mix. Grow in filtered or diffused light; likes moisture but soil should dry somewhat between waterings. New plants are started by rooting plantlets in sand. Chlorophytums are fine basket plants, but they are equally good in pots where they do well when potbound. Shift to larger container when roots seem about to heave the plant up and out of the pot. *C. comosum* (Figure 62) and *C. elatum* are recommended.

CHRYSANTHEMUMS. 45–60 F

Probably no flowering plant grown and loved today has a richer history than the chrysanthemum. Oriental in origin, it has been a symbol of Chinese culture for more than two thousand years. Introduced to Europe in the late 1600's, it found its way to the United States about 1800, and interest in its development and cultivation increased until today (Color Plate V) it is surpassed only by the geranium as the favorite pot plant.

Chrysanthemums grown under glass normally flower during October, November, and December. However, manipulation of light and temperature can cause normally short-day chrysanthemums to flower at any season you desire. Long nights of winter set and develop buds in nature, so by covering the plants with dark cloth from 5 p.m. to 8 a.m. you can initiate early budding. Conversely, if days are lengthened with artificial light, flowering can be delayed. Growth patterns may be further altered by pinching on a special time schedule that relates to bud formation, and by disbudding. If you plan to specialize in chrysanthemums, cultural directions covering these and other interesting and important procedures should be studied carefully.

Chrysanthemums like a loose, fibrous soil rich in organic matter—at least one-fourth coarse peatmoss or well-rotted manure. Roots must have an adequate supply of oxygen and soil must be well drained, especially if plants are grown in pots. Soil used in the mixture must be sterilized to prevent the fungus of verticillium wilt from attacking the plants.

Bud development for normal fall flowering takes place from about the 15th to 25th of August. During bud formation, night temperature should be lowered gradually, down to 56 F if possible; a lower temperature than this, however, causes bud development to cease or no buds to develop at all.

Chrysanthemums grow to considerable height, so stems must be supported. If you specialize in and devote your entire greenhouse to chrysanthemums, a bench wiring frame installation is necessary. Frames should be set up when plants are quite short so support will be available to assure straightness as stems elongate. Otherwise, individual stakes of wire or bamboo are satisfactory; fasten stems to the support at regular intervals with string or plant ties.

Buy rooted cuttings from your local garden center or order from a mail-order firm that specializes in chrysanthemums. Space cuttings sufficiently far apart in bench to allow free movement of air. Mulch with peatmoss during summer to keep soil moist, especially if cuttings are benched early in May (necessary with some varieties). Take care to set cuttings into the bench only to the depth they previously grew in the rooting medium. Daily misting encourages growth and prevents wilting of newly benched cuttings.

Fertilizer is not necessary until buds begin to form; then a liquid fertilizer application every two weeks is beneficial until color appears in buds.

After your first season of growing chrysanthemums, you might like to make your own cuttings. Place a few stock plants in a cool section of the greenhouse. Water sparingly and do not crowd. As the warmer, brighter days of early spring approach, growth will resume. Take cuttings from this new growth from April through June, depending on the varieties. Cut or break 3 to 5 inches of tip growth, insert in sand, peat and sand, or perlite. A root-promoting powder may be used if desired, but most chrysanthemums produce roots within three weeks whether so treated or not. Transplant as soon as roots have developed, and shift as required to prevent plants from becoming potbound.

There are so many varieties of chrysanthemums, and such variations of colors and kinds, it would be difficult to suggest a list. Growers' catalogues furnish complete descriptions and color groupings from which you can make your own selections.

Chrysanthemum frutescens (marguerite; Boston-yellow-daisy), and

Chrysanthemum Parthenium (feverfew) are grown according to the same cultural suggestions given above for chrysanthemums.

CLERODENDRUM. GLORY-BOWER. 60–70 F

A warm-greenhouse vine that flowers freely when confined to a hanging basket or a pot. Large loose clusters of brilliant scarlet, red, or white blossoms appear when plant is only 18 inches high. Seeds or cuttings are started in January in a mixture of sand and peat, then potted in a mixture of loam, leafmold, and sand. Apply liquid fertilizer regularly and keep soil evenly moist, for almost continuous flowering starting in April. Shade during summer. After flowering, reduce water and reduce temperature to 55 F. Keep on dry side until growth cycle begins again in January; then increase water and fertilizer to force blooms for spring. Clerodendrum foliage is coarse and emits an unpleasant odor when disturbed or touched, but probably you will never notice this undesirable characteristic. The attractive flowers are usually delightfully fragrant. Recommended: *C. Bungei,* heady fragrance similar to that of nicotiana; *C. fragrans pleniflorum* (cashmere-bouquet); and *C. Thomsoniae* (bleeding-heart-vine).

CLIVIA miniata. KAFIR-LILY. 50–65 F

Orange-yellow trumpet-shaped blossoms are borne in clusters atop a thick spike, usually held well above the straplike waxy evergreen leaves. Mine, a gift, was potted in a large pot and had considerable foliage. Being crowded for space, I placed it on an upturned box at the heater end of the greenhouse where the temperature remained at about 55 F. In February, when new growth was evident, I watered well and used a fish oil fertilizer about every three weeks. When I saw the flower bud and spike nestled at the base of the leaves, I moved the plant up into the brighter area but shaded it from direct sun. It remained there during March while it bloomed, then was returned to its spot by the heater. The fleshy roots resent disturbance, but they do crowd the container after a few years and repotting becomes necessary. Use a mix of garden loam, clean sharp sand, and peatmoss. Foliage continues to develop during summer. November through December is a normal resting period, so hold back on water somewhat, but never let clivia dry out completely, and do not cut away the foliage as you would with its relative, amaryllis. Inspect for mealy bugs in the tight areas where leaves curl around center growth. Propagate by seeds (six to seven years to first bloom), or by dividing large, multiple-crowned plants in January or just after March flowering.

CODIAEUM variegatum. CROTON.   60–75 F

Splashes of brilliant color to relieve the monotonous green of a greenhouse devoted to foliage plants. Broad flat or narrow twisted leaves are splashed or speckled with myriad hues and shades of pink, red, yellow, purple-brown, and cream. Grow crotons in mix of equal parts garden loam, clean sharp sand, and humus or leafmold, with a little well-rotted manure added. Keep moist at all times except when plants are resting. Good drainage is required. Keep crotons out of direct sun; semishade is ideal, especially during summer. Seeds started in moist sphagnum moss almost any time of year usually germinate in about 30 days. Six-inch tip cuttings may be rooted from March to June.

COLEUS Blumei.   50–70 F

Rich, colorful foliage furnishes a riot of color: combinations of red-yellow, yellow-green, red-green, and several others. A single plant pinched often as it matures will grow to tremendous size. Remove flowers whenever they appear so seed will not set on plant. Coleus is not fussy as to soil, but is susceptible to mealy bug. Plants wilt quickly if soil is not evenly moist. Propagate by seeds sown in spring (germination two to three weeks in 70 F); or you can root cuttings from mature plants quickly and easily in sand or water.

CRINUM.   55–65 F

Crinums incline to rather large growth, so one or two will be sufficient for a small greenhouse. Six to twelve fragrant lily-like blossoms appear atop a thick stalk of this plant that grows from a tender bulb. Flowers are excitingly colorful, ranging from pure white to pink through purple, and red in hybrids. Water about the first of the year to induce growth; blooms start in spring and continue through summer. A soil mix of garden loam and well-rotted manure with some sand added for good drainage suits crinums very well; they like to be kept moist and must have good drainage. Provide summer shade. Feed with liquid fertilizer every two to three weeks during growth. Plants may be dried off and rested dry under benches after flowering, or continued in growth for their attractive foliage. Recommended: *C. americanum* (swamp-lily), white flowers; *C. longifolium*, white or pink flowers; *C. Moorei*, rose-red flowers.

CROSSANDRA infundibuliformis. 55–70 F

This evergreen plant has attractive glossy, waxy, gardenia-like leaves, almost everblooming flowers of overlapping petals of bright salmon color. Grow in mix of equal parts of rich loam, peat, and clean sharp sand. Seeds are slow and uncertain to germinate, but 3-inch tip cuttings root readily in moist sand with bottom heat and high humidity.

CYCLAMEN indicum (formerly *C. persicum*). 45–55 F

No cool greenhouse should be without at least one cyclamen. Recent hybrids (Color Plate I and Figure 63) are larger, more beautiful, in a range of colors from pure white through rose, pink, salmon, to scarlet and orchid. There are single, double, and fringed blossoms, even a pleasingly scented miniature-flowered variety. Flowers appear in profusion for up to six months, sometimes longer, hiding dark green

63. Cyclamen. (GEORGE W. PARK SEED CO. PHOTO)

foliage, standing stiffly on rosy-hued tubular stems, not unlike tremendous butterflies poised in flight.

Buy your first cyclamen (select a large, heavily budded plant) from your florist or garden center in November. Keep the plant cool and moist and shade it from direct sun at midday; feed every other week. When flowering ceases in April or May, force the plant to rest by withholding water until foliage dies. Keep nearly dry in the pot on its side under a bench until August. Then remove dead foliage and some of the old soil from around the rootball and repot in fresh soil (equal parts garden loam, peatmoss, sand) in a pot slightly larger than the rootball, and with good drainage. Be especially careful to keep the top of the tuber level with the surface of the soil—if it is set lower, water may collect in the indentation and cause crown rot. Syringe daily. Grow at 50 F night temperature and provide adequate ventilation. Remove all flower buds that appear before October. Cyclamens may be grown from seed planted from June to September, but it takes fifteen to eighteen months to produce flowering plants this way. Allow five to eight weeks for germination—a tiny tuber develops under the soil before leaves appear above. Cyclamens are intolerant of some pesticides, so read instructions carefully before treating.

DAHLIAS.   45–70 F

With so many interesting miniature varieties available, it might be fun to try a few dahlias in the greenhouse. Seeds sown in February germinate rapidly in sphagnum moss. When seedlings are large enough to handle, transplant to 3-inch pots in soil rich in humus. Plants grow rapidly and, if not crowded, do not require pinching to induce branching. Shift to larger pots as necessary. Buds set in a few weeks, and if given plenty of sun will start flowering in early summer. You can also propagate dahlias by dividing tubers in February, placing the divisions in moist sand with bottom heat until leaves appear and plants are large enough to handle. Transfer to 3-inch pots and treat same as seedlings. Recommended: 'Early Bird', extra double dwarf; 'Fall Festival'; Coltness Hybrids.

DIANTHUS Caryophyllus. CARNATION.   45–50 F

The colors and spicy fragrance make carnations a "must" for the hobbyist who wants flowers for cutting. The continuing supply of blooms over several months from an area 5 feet long by the width of the bench will be richly rewarding. Purchase cuttings from your florist or garden center, preferably in December—cuttings taken early seem to root best. Dip cut ends in root-promoting powder and insert in sand in a flat or cutting bed with bottom heat. Usually the root system is sufficiently large in three weeks to transplant to the bench. Bench soil should be a mixture of equal parts sand, leafmold, and garden loam, plus a little superphosphate. Ideal benching distance is from 6 to 10 inches apart, but with space at such a premium, I crowd mine to 4 inches and grow them without pinching. When transplanting, set at same level in the soil as previously planted, otherwise stem rot may result. Carnations like plenty of ventilation, bright sunshine, and a cool temperature. For December cuttings no fertilizer will be necessary until February, then apply 4-12-4 fertilizer for the next three months. Carnations should be supported during their entire growth with bench wiring frames or similar arrangements. Disbudding is recommended to allow one bud to develop to a large size by removing all other buds on the stem, but I suggest this be done with only about half the stems, as the side buds furnish blossoms of various sizes ideal for floral arrangements. If you select one or two plants for growing on as stock plants, you will have your own supply of cutting material to start your next crop. Stock plants should be pinched heavily until September to induce side branching. Recommended: 'Marguerite', fully double flowers in wide range of colors, excellent for cutting, blooms in five months from seed: 'Chabaud', large, fragrant, double apricot-orange striped and flushed with scarlet; 'Petite Pink', the first miniature F_1 hybrid carnation, fully double, deliciously fragrant 2-inch flowers on long wiry stems.

ESCHSCHOLZIA californica. CALIFORNIA-POPPY.   45–50 F

One of the most unusual flowering plants I ever tried in my greenhouse. Lovely, lacy foliage bursts with an endless procession of moderate-size poppies in dazzling shades of yellow through brilliant orange, and bicolors of rose and white, scarlet and amber. Sow seeds directly onto bench soil where plants are to grow; cull to avoid crowding when plants are 2 inches high. You can have a rewarding display in only 2 feet of bench space, as these poppies are everblooming. (This plant's name is frequently misspelled "Eschscholtzia" in catalogues.)

EUCHARIS grandiflora. AMAZON-LILY.   **60–70 F**

Few tender bulbs produce flowers to rival the beauty and delicious fragrance of this dazzling white amaryllid. Clusters of 3-inch blossoms on long thick stalks appear in late winter and early spring, but bulbs can be brought to flower practically any time of year by withholding water for several weeks, watering only enough to keep foliage from dying off completely. Pot in mix of three parts fibrous loam and 1 part well-rotted manure, with sand added to provide good drainage, since eucharis likes plenty of water while growing. Provide full sun during winter but some protection during summer. Syringe frequently to control mealy bugs and thrips. Repot only when necessary as plants grow best when roots are not disturbed. Bulbs can be separated for propagation during spring, but growth will be checked; if propagation is attempted, water sparingly until new growth is evident.

EUPHORBIA pulcherrima. POINSETTIA.   **60–65 F**

If you can purchase a few rooted cuttings, you will enjoy growing both red and white poinsettias to flower at Christmas. Pot rooted cuttings in 2½- or 3-inch pots in soil mix of three parts garden loam, one part clean sharp sand, and one part well-rotted manure. Water thoroughly; place in shade out of direct sunlight until they become established; mist or syringe lightly several times a day. Pinching to induce branching will produce more than one blossom per plant. A hard pinch (removing entire top of plant including several leaves) should be made no later than August first; a soft pinch (removing tip only) can be made August 15. When plants outgrow small pots, repot singly, or several to a 6- or 8-inch pot. Water thoroughly after repotting. Maintain temperature at 60 F, avoid drafts, and water moderately. Too much or too little water, sudden changes in temperature, or drafts cause foliage to drop. Color should be evident by November fifteenth. Apply a complete fertilizer every two to three weeks after color appears, and full color should be attained by Christmas. Poinsettias set buds between October tenth and twentieth—take care not to expose plants to artificial light during these ten days; otherwise, you may have no flowers. After flowering, plants may be carried on as stock plants to furnish cuttings for the next season. Place pots on sides in a 50 to 55 F temperature until April; cut back to 8 inches and repot. Raise temperature to 60 or 65 F and syringe and water frequently. One ounce of ammonium sulfate dissolved in two gallons of water helps at this time. Anytime May to August make 4- to 6-inch cuttings, preferably in the morning. Place them in water for an hour to retard loss of milky juice, then pot directly in 2½- or 3-inch pots, or root in sand first. Water thoroughly to firm soil around cutting. Place shade some distance above cuttings to allow free air circulation, and syringe or mist several times a day for about ten days.

EUPHORBIA splendens. CROWN-OF-THORNS.   **60–65 F**

This unusual plant prefers a warm greenhouse, but I have been successful with one in my 52 F house. Long fleshy stems, laden with spines and tiny bright green oval leaves, produce scarlet-orange bracts practically all year. Stems, though thick, are easily trained on wire supports into interesting shapes. Crown-of-thorns may shed practically all its leaves in late fall and early winter while continuing to bloom, replacing the leaves as spring approaches. Clusters of bracts are more numerous in winter, though it is practically everblooming. Grow in full sun. Cuttings are easy to root in moist sand—let the cut portions dry in open air for an hour or so before inserting—and will bloom when only a few inches high. *E. Bojeri* (Figure 64) is similar to *E. splendens.*

64. *Euphorbia Bojeri.* (MERRY GARDENS PHOTO)

65. *Felicia amelloides.*

FELICIA amelloides. BLUE-MARGUERITE.   50–60 F

Star-shaped, sky-blue flowers with yellow centers (Figure 65)—this is one of the truly blue flowers. Sow seed in September in equal parts garden loam and leafmold for March blooming. Pinch several times before buds appear to induce branching and fullness. Several plants to a 7-inch pot provide plenty of blooms to cut for bouquets without spoiling the appearance of the plant. Felicias are also easily propagated from cuttings in May or June.

FERNS.   45–70 F

If you would forego the beauty, color, and fragrance of flowering plants to pursue a fascinating hobby under glass, consider ferns (see Figures 41, 66–70). The filmy, feathery, or leathery leaves or fronds are so interesting they could command your complete attention. Kinds are numerous, all are unusual, even the names are intriguing.

Most ferns grow best at temperatures above 50 F; they are about evenly divided between the intermediate range of 50–55 F and the warm range of 65–70 F, but there are several that grow nicely in a cool greenhouse at 45–50 F. All prefer humus-rich soil that retains moisture but drains well. Use a mix of loam, a little well-rotted manure, and leafmold or peatmoss, plus some horticultural charcoal or coarse sand, even broken crock or granite chips, to assure good drainage. The atmosphere in the greenhouse must be warm and humid, with filtered sunlight or complete shading. Pay close attention to ventilation, for ferns resent drafts. A monthly feeding of fish emulsion promotes rich, lush green foliage. Keep evenly moist except when resting. Ferns may be grown in pots, but when planted in hanging baskets they are not only shown off to best advantage, but lend a decorative, ethereal air to your greenhouse garden.

Following are brief descriptions of a few ferns you will enjoy in the greenhouse:

Adiantum tenerum, maidenhair-fern, 60–65 F. This popular plant with lacy fronds and compact growth habit (Figure 66) prefers to be grown out of direct sun and in high humidity. The humusy soil should never be allowed to dry out.

Asparagus plumosus, asparagus-fern, 50–55 F. A dark green fluffy, needled fern popular for use in bouquets. *A. Sprengeri* is a little coarser and has small white flowers followed by red berries.

66. *Adiantum Wrightii.* (MERRY GARDENS PHOTO)

67. *Davallia Mariesii.*
(MERRY GARDENS PHOTO)

68. *Nephrolepis exaltata* 'Verona'.
(MERRY GARDENS PHOTO)

69. *Platycerium Stemaria.*
(MERRY GARDENS PHOTO)

70. *Pteris ensiformis Victoriae.*
(MERRY GARDENS PHOTO)

Asplenium bulbiferum, mother-fern, 50–55 F. Particularly beautiful in hanging baskets; fuzzy brown stems and dark green, gracefully curving fronds. Tiny plantlets are produced on upper surfaces of fronds. These soon produce fronds of their own, and when several have developed they may be separated from the mother plant and placed in a closed container (glass-covered casserole, pot covered with plastic bag, anything that will maintain a moist, humid atmosphere) until large enough to be potted.

Asplenium Nidus (formerly called *A. Nidus-Avis*), bird's-nest-fern, 50–55 F. Fronds are broad and glossy green, growing in a rosette resembling the nest of a bird. Never allow soil to dry.

Davallia Mariesii (formerly *D. bullata*), a squirrel's-foot-fern, 50–65 F. The rhizome of this interesting fern (Figure 67) is fuzzy, brown, and creeping in character. Fine lacy fronds grow from the woolly rhizome.

Platycerium bifurcatum, staghorn-fern, 50–55 F. Interesting, quite different from the general run of ferns with its long forked foliage resembling the flat branching horns of a stag, it lends itself well to hanging baskets, especially those made of redwood slats filled with osmunda fiber or sphagnum moss mixed with charcoal for drainage. *P. Stemaria*, triangle staghorn-fern, is shown in Figure 69.

Polystichum adiantiforme, leather-fern, 50–55 F. While the fronds have the general graceful feathery shape associated with most ferns, they are actually thick, glossy, and leathery and produce a bushy plant from brown furry rhizomes.

Pteris ensiformis Victoriae, sword brake-fern, 50–65 F. Short graceful fronds of silver and green (Figure 70). In spring, cut off all dead fronds and repot.

FREESIA.   50–55 F

No greenhouse should be without the fragrance of a pot or two of freesias, even though the foliage is unattractive and plants must be supported. Corms produce terminal clusters of small trumpet-like light-blue, yellow, or creamy white blossoms at the ends of tall spikes. Plant corms in shallow bulb-pans or seed flats in a mix of three parts garden loam, one part leafmold, peatmoss or well-rotted manure. Corms, shaped like teardrops, should be planted with the pointed end up, pressed into the soil with tips just showing. Water thoroughly when planted, then sparingly until top growth is established. Pots can be kept under the bench for a while before being brought up into full light, if space is at a premium. Freesias like a night temperature of 50 F, plenty of air circulation, and full sun except during extremely hot periods. Corms planted from August to November will provide flowers from December through March. After flowering, let foliage die off gradually, remove corms from soil and store in a cool dry place until time to replant in the fall. Freesias can also be grown from seed, but corms are much the easier way.

FUCHSIA. LADY'S-EAR-DROPS.   **45–50 F**

Trailing fuchsias are ideal for hanging baskets; upright types are grown as pot plants or developed as standards. No longer are you lim-

71. Super Giant Freesia. (GEORGE W. PARK SEED CO. PHOTO)

72. Fuchsia. (GEORGE W. PARK SEED CO. PHOTO)

ited to the purple-red blossoms of the species—you may indulge your fancy for colors from white through pink to red, orange, orchid, even blue, and for single or double flowers.

Fuchsias like a cool temperature and a humid atmosphere, but unless air circulation is adequate, there may be trouble with fungous diseases. The plants are not extremely fussy in their light requirements and will do well in full sun or light shade except during summer, when they must be shaded lightly. They require a lot of water when in active growth, which means soil must be kept moist. Planting mix must be coarse enough to allow excellent drainage. Try a mix of equal parts leafmold, garden loam, well-rotted manure, and add a small amount of clean sharp sand to aid drainage. Feed regularly every two weeks while in active growth—fish emulsion is good.

Fuchsias may be summered in the greenhouse, or outdoors under lath or other light shade. When returning to the greenhouse in fall, let plants rest for a month by keeping them almost dry. Then remove from pots, scrape away some of the old soil, and repot in the same size pot in fresh soil.

A fuchsia standard, or tree, is not difficult to grow and the result is well worth the little extra attention required. Transfer a well-rooted cutting to a 6- or 7-inch pot. When it is growing well, stake it to insure a straight sturdy stem. Rub off side shoots as they appear and allow only the main stem to grow until it reaches the desired height. Then pinch so the top will become a many-branched, bushy head. Pinch at intervals as growth continues, and you will have a nicely shaped standard in about two years.

Fuchsias to be used in hanging baskets should be trailing varieties that are self-branching. If self-branching kinds are not available, pinch other trailing types to encourage branching.

Propagate fuchsias by cuttings taken anytime from October through March and rooted in moist sand. Transfer rooted cuttings to 2½-inch pots and grow them slightly warmer than mature plants, about 52 to 55 F until well established. The next move is to a 4- or 5-inch pot; or, for full bushy specimens, place three plants in a 6-inch pot and pinch. Pinched plants flower seven or eight weeks after the last pinch. Fuchsias may be grown from seed—interesting, because the seeds do not always come true and you may grow a new or unusual form.

Fuchsias are susceptible to several pests—white flies, mealy bugs, thrips, and red spiders—and should be sprayed regularly.

GARDENIA jasminoides.   65–70 F

Glossy green foliage and fragrant waxy-white flowers are worth the effort necessary to grow gardenias successfully. Night temperature of 65 F and high humidity must be maintained; drafts and sudden temperature changes must be avoided. Keep soil moist at all times, syringe foliage frequently. Give full sun. Additional (artificial) light from mid-September will encourage a longer blooming period. Purchase your first gardenia from a florist or garden center. If you are successful in growing it, take 4- to 6-inch tip cuttings to increase your supply. Cuttings, dipped in root-promoting powder, require bottom heat and a humid atmosphere and are best started from December through March, in sand; they should be well rooted in four to six weeks, then they are ready for 2½- or 3-inch pots. Equal parts of soil and acid peat plus a small amount of superphosphate make a good potting mix. Soil must be acid. Every two to three weeks, apply 1 ounce of iron sulphate dissolved in 2 gallons of water. Vinegar (½ teaspoon to a quart of water) also helps to maintain the acidity required. Shift to larger pots as necessary—gardenias should not be potbound. About every six weeks use a complete liquid fertilizer in place of the iron sulphate or vinegar solutions. To prevent the bud drop caused by low humidity, syringe foliage and wet down walks frequently during hot weather. Small-leaved large-flowered *G. jasminoides Veitchii* blooms intermittently through the year.

GESNERIADS.   60–65 F

You could devote several greenhouses exclusively to gesneriads and still not have enough space. The best known gesneriads are African-violets (*Saintpaulia*) and gloxinias (*Sinningia*) but at least forty other genera, each with from one to countless species and hybrids, are popular warm-greenhouse plants. General requirements are a very porous well-drained potting medium, relative humidity of 45 to 55 per cent, excellent air circulation around the plants but no direct drafts, regular fertilizing while plants are in growth, water frequently enough to keep the medium moist but not soggy, prompt removal of fading flowers and deteriorating foliage, and (ideally) enough space so plants do not

73. *Kohleria amabilis,* a rhizomatous gesneriad that blooms steadily for six or more months, at the same time prodigiously multiplying the number of rhizomes in the pot. (MERRY GARDENS PHOTO)

touch each other. This family, *Gesneriaceae,* includes tuberous-rooted plants as *Chrysothemis,* ✕*Gloxinera, Rechsteineria,* and *Sinningia* (Color Plate I); rhizomatous-rooted plants as *Achimenes, Diastema,* ✕*Eucodonopsis, Gloxinia perennis, Koellikeria, Kohleria* (Color Plate IV and Figure 73), and *Smithiantha* (Figure 74); and fibrous-rooted, usually evergreen, plants as *Aeschynanthus, Chirita, Codonanthe, Columnea, Episcia, Hypocyrta, Nautilocalyx, Nematanthus, Saintpaulia* (Color Plate II), and *Streptocarpus* (Figure 75).

GLADIOLUS.   50–60 F

Garden-type gladiolus can be flowered in the greenhouse during spring from corms planted in February, but I prefer the baby or winter-flowering types that provide color and fragrance during bleak February days, from corms planted in November. Use a mix of garden loam, humus, and sand, in pots large enough to plant several corms 1 inch

74. *Smithiantha multiflora,* a rhizomatous gesneriad. Smithianthas bloom in fall, have stunningly colored velvety-textured foliage. (MERRY GARDENS PHOTO)

75. Streptocarpus hybrid, one of the fibrous-rooted gesneriads. (MERRY GARDENS PHOTO)

deep and 1 inch apart. Water well to settle corms into soil, then water sparingly until growth starts. Stems about 2 feet high produce three to five blossoms; colors may be white, pink, or red. After blooming, keep foliage growing until it dies back naturally. Clean and store corms for the next season. Offsets can be potted as new corms, but they must grow for several seasons to develop into corms sufficiently large to produce flowers. Recommended: *G. tristis,* delightfully fragrant yellowish-white flowers; *G.* ×*Colvillei,* small, very early scarlet flowers.

GLORIOSA Rothschildiana. GLORY-LILY.   55–65 F

A climbing lily of dramatic beauty with golden-crimson blossoms toned cream at the base and with slender, backward-curving petals. Plant in equal-thirds mix of garden loam, leafmold, and sand. The long tubers require a deep pot; plant one to a 6-inch pot or three to an 8-inch pot in January for blooms starting in March. When blooming ceases, foliage gradually dies off. Tubers should be stored dry until time to start the next growing cycle, when they should be repotted in fresh soil. Also recommended: *G. superba,* flowers yellow-orange changing to red; *G. virescens,* bright red or yellow flowers.

GYNURA aurantiaca. VELVET-PLANT.   **60–65 F**

A most unusual plant—fleshy leaves are densely covered with very fine violet or purple hairs that make the leaves look velvety. Grows well in garden soil with decayed manure and peat or humus added. Bright light or full sun is required to bring out the color in the foliage, but the plant grows well in diffused light. Except during the resting period, gynura should be kept evenly moist, but do not overwater. If your plant grows too large and sprawly, start new plants from tip cuttings rooted in sand.

GYPSOPHILA elegans. BABY'S-BREATH.   **45–50 F**

A flat or two of this airy annual is indispensable to provide delicate blossoms for flower arrangements. To have a continuous crop, sow seeds in December (germination five days) and repeat about every two weeks through April. In winter it takes about three months from seed to bloom (earlier winter flowering can be hastened somewhat by the use of artificial light); toward spring, a month less is required. Color forms of this species are available with white, rose, or crimson flowers.

HAEMANTHUS. BLOOD-LILY.   **50–60 F**

Another very unusual lily-like plant (Color Plate IV)—a single thick stalk about a foot high terminates in a ball of thin red spikes, resembling a pincushion. Flower spikes may appear before or after foliage. The tender bulbs like a rich fibrous loam mixed with sand. Do not cover the bulb but leave the top just visible above the soil. Once established, growth is delayed if roots are disturbed, so plan to grow in the same pot for several years. When growth appears, replace an inch or two of the topsoil with fresh soil. This will be in either spring or fall, depending on the species. Water sparingly at first, but as plant grows, give plenty of water, and liquid fertilizer on a regular 2-week schedule. After blooming, bulbs become dormant. Withhold most moisture then, allowing just enough to keep bulbs from shriveling. Recommended: *H. coccineus,* scarlet flower in fall before foliage; *H. Katharinae,* red flower in spring after foliage, evergreen.

HEDERA Helix. ENGLISH IVY.   **45–50 F**

This all-time favorite makes an attractive shelf plant or bench edging, and looks well combined with ivy-leaved geraniums, lobelia, or low-growing ageratum or candytuft in a hanging basket. The equal thirds mixture of garden soil, loam, peatmoss; bright light or full sun; good air circulation; and evenly moist but not soggy soil are the simple requirements.

HELIOTROPIUM arborescens. HELIOTROPE. 55–65 F

Try some of these old-fashioned favorites (Figure 76) in your greenhouse. White, lavender, or dark violet-blue flowers are delightfully fragrant. Blossoms appear in large clusters on stems 15 to 24 inches long in the dwarf varieties. Heliotropes like rich soil and prefer night temperature of 60 F to grow, though 68 F minimum is necessary to germinate seed, which takes three to four weeks. Cuttings can be taken from mature plants; they root readily in moist sand. Recommended: 'Marine', semi-dwarf variety with dark violet-blue flowers; 'First Snow', pure white flowers; 'Blue Bonnet', deepest blue.

HIPPEASTRUM. AMARYLLIS. 55–65 F

Flowers are breathtakingly beautiful, pure white through shades of pink and red, three to four huge 8-inch flowers to a stem that is about 2 feet tall. For February and March bloom, plant in late October; for summer bloom you can plant as late as March. If you want amaryllis flowers for Christmas, buy one of the prepared Dutch bulbs or a South

76. *Heliotropium arborescens.* (MERRY GARDENS PHOTO)

African amaryllis that blooms naturally about December 25. Plant each bulb in fibrous loam (1 part each soil, sand, peat) in a pot large enough to allow about an inch of soil between bulb and pot wall. Center a bulb in the pot, with one-third to one-half of the bulb protruding above the soil line. Water thoroughly once, sparingly thereafter until growth starts; then gradually increase water and move plant to a sunny place. Flower stem usually gets quite tall and flowers may open before foliage appears. After bloom is finished, it is important to keep plants growing so bulbs will develop properly and make embryo flowers for next year. This is the time to water freely and fertilize about every two weeks until leaves show signs of dying down in late summer. Then gradually dry off plants and store pots in a cool but above-freezing place. Some bulbs will soon indicate that a new cycle is commencing; others must be started into growth in October or November by moving pots to warmer quarters and watering.

77. Amaryllis (*Hippeastrum*). (GEORGE W. PARK SEED CO. PHOTO)

HYMENOCALLIS calathina. PERUVIAN-DAFFODIL. **55–60 F**

Richly scented lily-like flowers of unusual character. Two-foot stems support four or five pure white fringed, cup-shaped blossoms with green striped throat, each surrounded by five slender curving petals. Foliage is dark green, sword shaped. Plant bulbs in spring in mix of equal parts soil, sand, peatmoss or manure. Water well once, then sparingly until growth is well established. Increase watering until after blooming, which usually occurs in early summer. Keep foliage growing after blooming. Gradually withhold water starting in September. Dry off bulbs and store in a cool dry place until spring. If proper care is given, bulbs may be grown for several years. *H. calathina sulphurea,* also called 'Sulphur Queen', is primrose yellow with deep yellow-and-green striped throat.

IMPATIENS. TOUCH-ME-NOT. **55–65 F**

For an old-time favorite in modern dress, try one or two of the new dwarf varieties. They prefer a temperature a little on the warm side, plenty of fresh air, and good light, though some of the newer varieties do well in shady areas. Seeds of impatiens are temperamental about germinating—they are sensitive to low temperature and a minimum of 70 F is necessary for germination. Sow seeds on moist sphagnum moss August first for winter bloom. Transplant to a mix of peatmoss, manure, and garden loam. Keep evenly moist but do not allow soil to become water-logged. Fertilize biweekly. Impatiens may also be propagated by cuttings.

IRIS. **55–60 F**

With a careful selection of winter-flowering kinds, blooms can be had from Christmas through April. Plant bulbs in good garden soil in deep flats or pots, or directly into bench. Insufficient water is the major problem with iris culture—if soil dries out at any time, there will probably be no flowers. Take care also not to injure roots. Iris require plenty of air circulation and light, so space bulbs 2 to 3 inches apart and cover with at least 1 inch of soil. If your bulbs have not been precooled, pot them by mid-September and store at 50 F for six weeks for early flowering, or bury in a well-drained area outside the greenhouse. Bring into greenhouse about November 15th and raise temperature to 58 F. If the familiar Wedgewood blue iris is treated in this manner, flowers will be available for Christmas, from the largest size bulbs. Smaller bulbs will flower later. Precooled bulbs should be potted or benched in mid-October. After flowering, water moderately until foliage dies back, clean bulbs and store for use the following season.

KALANCHOE.   50–70 F

Many species of this attractive succulent (Color Plate IV) are available to the greenhouse gardener. Foliage may be arrow-shaped, notched, or curled; flowers yellowish-green, creamy-white, coral-pink to scarlet-red. Sow seeds in March for flowering plants by Christmas. Shade from 5 p.m. to 7 a.m. from August 15th until October. Transplant to 2½-, then to 4-inch pots in mix of two parts garden loam, one part peatmoss. Provide good drainage, keep moderately moist. Occasional dilute solutions of liquid fertilizer promote stocky compact growth. Mealy bugs are a real problem. Inspect frequently for this pest, treat immediately with swabs dipped in alcohol. If you cannot control the infestation, destroy the plant. Do not use DDT; it may seriously injure or kill the plant. Recommended: *K. beharensis* (velvet-leaf-plant), yellowish-green flowers, fuzzy leaves and stem; *K. Fedtschenkoi marginata tricolor* (aurora-borealis), gray, white, pink; *K. scandens* (mobile-plant), wiry blackish-green foliage on trailing stems, purple tubular blooms; 'Scarlet Gnome', bright scarlet flowers on 7-inch symmetrical plants.

LACHENALIA. CAPE-COWSLIP.   50 F

The tiny, tender, teardrop-shaped bulbs should be planted about 1 inch apart, point up, and covered very lightly with soil. After summer heat is over, plant in a mix of two parts garden loam, one part peatmoss or humus, one part sand, and place in a coldframe until growth is well started. Then move in to a cool 50 F greenhouse (flower buds will not form in high temperature) and keep moist. Bell-shaped blossoms, appearing for several months starting December, hang in rows from the top half of 10-inch stems. If you have no coldframe you may find, as I have, that keeping pots in the dark under the greenhouse bench until shoots are about 2 inches high, then bringing them up into the light, works as well. Keep foliage growing for a while after flowering, then gradually withhold water until soil is completely dry. Leave bulbs in pots until the next growing season, then repot in fresh soil. Be extremely careful when repotting, as many very tiny offsets will have developed— these can be potted to increase your supply of this interesting flowering plant. Recommended: *L. contaminata,* white flowers; *L. purpureo-caerulea,* blue-purple flowers; *L. tricolor,* red-tipped yellow flowers.

LANTANA. 50–60 F

Either the shrubby or trailing type can be used in baskets, but the trailer with lavender flowers (*L. montevidensis*) makes the most attractive display. Blossoms of dwarf forms of the garden lantana (*L. Camara*) are white, bright yellow, or pink. Lantanas grow well in a cool greenhouse, but 60 F is best for continuous flowering. Use a slightly sandy soil and let plants get moderately dry between waterings. Fertilize frequently, grow in full sun or light shade, and cut back as necessary to keep plants within bounds.

LATHYRUS odoratus. SWEET-PEA. 45–50 F

Heat-resistant climbing types, and bush types specially developed for bench growing rather than ground beds, make it possible to grow this delightful cut flower in a small greenhouse. Seeds are available for winter-flowering and spring-flowering varieties which have been developed to produce true commercial-type large, long-stemmed, deliciously fragrant flowers in almost any color: white, pink, salmon, rose-cream to crimson, even dark blue. Dwarf varieties specially developed for shallow planting make it possible to grow sweet-peas in benches or pots. Sweet-peas are a cool crop; they must have plenty of ventilation to keep the temperature under 65 F during the day if possible. Water well in sunny weather. Seeds germinate more readily if soaked in water overnight before sowing. Plant seeds directly in benches where they are to grow, in a mix of 3 parts garden loam and 1 part well-rotted manure. Plant a row across end of bench at gable end of greenhouse and provide strings or wire from bench to greenhouse roof to support the vines. When a vine reaches the roof, it may be slipped down the string to allow additional space for growing, or it may be pinched off to restrict growth. Seeds may be sown two or three to a peat pot; plant pots in the bench when a good root system has been established. Transplant the new dwarf types to a pot for growing as pot plants. The new heat-resistant varieties provide flowers into warm weather. For flowers in December, sow seed in September. An October sowing will provide cut flowers through May. When plants are at least 1 foot high, use a complete fertilizer about once a month, but only in sunny weather.

Overfertilizing in dull weather may cause buds to drop, as may over-watering and sudden changes in temperature. Do not crowd plants, provide good ventilation, and you will be rewarded with many blooms for cutting. Recommended: Cuthbertson's Floribunda Mixed, 5 to 6 blooms to a stem; 'Lois', rose-pink on white; 'Jimmy', best scarlet.

LILIUM. LILY.   50–60 F

All of us, I daresay, have been awed and inspired by the stateliness, simplicity, and haunting fragrance of lilies. Some of us have thought how nice it would be to have lilies at other times than Easter and have planted the bulbs outdoors where they have bloomed again in fall. Yet, it is easily possible to have lilies in flower during the cold and bleak days of winter in our gardens under glass.

It is particularly important, if we are to grow lilies successfully, to realize that lily bulbs never go dormant—there is always some evidence of life. Lily roots stay fleshy and alive even when plants have died back and lost their foliage, and it is a condition of successful flowering that roots be kept moist at all times.

Dealers suggest that you order lily bulbs early enough so they can be shipped just at your planting time, to avoid delay between digging and planting.

Lilies like plenty of water when in active growth and a rich, fibrous soil. Use a mix of good garden loam and leafmold, and add a little bonemeal for extra nourishment furnished slowly. Eight-inch pots are best, to allow for the exceptionally strong root growth and make it un-necessary to repot until the second year. A layer of pebbles, broken crock, or charcoal under the soil provides good drainage.

When bulbs have been potted, water gently and gradually increase water as foliage appears. Place in a cool location for about four to six weeks to develop a good root system, then move to a cool, shady location outdoors to promote top growth. Return to greenhouse before frost and raise temperature to 60 F to induce earlier flowering, though flowers will be as nice if grown more slowly at 50 F. When plants come into greenhouse, feed with liquid manure or other liquid fertilizer every 7 to 10 days. If yours are cold-storage lilies, place them in the greenhouse at 60 F immediately upon potting. Keep foliage growing after flowers die off to strengthen bulb for the next growth cycle. Remember, even after foliage dies, the bulb is still alive and needs light watering occasionally to preserve the roots. Lilies benefit from a top dressing of fresh soil before starting another growth cycle, but try not to disturb the roots unless absolutely necessary to move to a larger pot.

I think you will enjoy growing these true lilies:

Lilium auratum, goldband lily. Pot non-precooled bulbs in 5- or 6-inch pots in April for flowers in January. Grows 3 to 6 feet high, has fragrant white blossoms speckled in crimson around a yellow band.

Lilium candidum, Madonna lily. Stems 2 to 4 feet high, waxy white extremely fragrant flowers; one of the few lilies that can stand full sun without damage; differs slightly from others in that temperature should be no higher than 55 F. It will take a little longer than the usual 13 weeks after bringing into greenhouse for blossoms to appear because they do grow at a cooler temperature.

Lilium pumilum (formerly *L. tenuifolium*), coral lily. A smaller type, with stems about 2 feet high; may remain dormant through a second season before blooming if roots have dried out before planting. Blossoms are brilliant scarlet, sometimes light at the base. Avoid direct sun.

Lilium regale, royal, regal, or Easter lily. One of the most beautiful lilies, with its half-yellow half-white throat with undertones of pink, and purple midribs; grows 3 to 6 feet high. Allow about 15 weeks after bringing into greenhouse before blooming. Likes partial shade.

Lilium speciosum rubrum, showy Japanese lily. One of the most valuable lilies for forcing; pot precooled bulbs and hold at 60 F starting in September for bloom in about 10 weeks. Flowers are white at tips, coloring to rose-pink toward centers with deep red spots, usual delicate lily fragrance. Grow in partial shade.

Mid-Century Lilies. Grow at 55 F. The nice thing about these lilies is that bulbs are precooled before shipment and can be potted and placed in the greenhouse for forcing immediately ('Prosperity' is the only one that requires a special rooting period). They like a loose, porous soil mix of 2 parts each sandy loam and peatmoss or leafmold, and 1 part sand, and uniform moisture while growing. Shade lightly to prevent leaf scorching. Alternate feedings of nitrogen and a complete fertilizer at 10-day intervals are beneficial. Recommended: 'Enchantment', blazing orange; 'Croesus', golden yellow; 'Cinnabar', maroon red; 'Prosperity', lemon yellow.

LOBELIA Erinus.   50–55 F

This dainty plant seldom appears in lists of plants recommended
for growing under glass. The compact 4-inch high plants are covered
with irregularly shaped flowers of bright clear blue, white, or red;
foliage is delicate and lacy. It is an ideal edging plant for greenhouse
benches, or can be grown as a pot plant. Sow several seeds in peat pots
containing a mix of 1 part each sand, leafmold, and garden loam; do not
cover seed. When plants are established, sink the peat pots to their
tops in bench soil about 6 inches apart; space 10 inches apart if they
are to be combined with other edging plants. Lobelias do best in semi-
shade; pinch to get full, shapely plants. Recommended: 'Blue Stone',
4-inch compact plant with small bright blue flowers; 'White Lady',
5-inch plant, white flowers; 'Rosamond', deep carmine red flowers with
white eye.

LOBULARIA maritima. SWEET-ALYSSUM.   45–50 F

Scented drifts of rich violet, rose-pink, or snowy white, separately or
combined, make lovely edgings for greenhouse benches or for home
display in small containers, teacups, or low bowls. Plants grow quickly
(germination 5 days) from seed sown any time of year; flowers appear
in about 4 weeks. Recommended: 'Carpet of Snow', white; 'Pink
Heather', soft lavender-pink; 'Violet King' or 'Violet Queen', rich
purple.

MANETTIA. FIRECRACKER-VINE.   55–60 F

Fast-growing vine that climbs on anything it touches, good as trellis
or rafter vine in the greenhouse. Many yellow-tipped red flowers pop
out all over twining threadlike stems. If pruned ruthlessly, manettias
may be grown as bushy pot plants. Grow in all-purpose medium;
propagate by cuttings or seeds. Recommended: *M. bicolor, M. glabra.*

MATHIOLA incana. STOCK.   45–50 F

One of my favorite bench plants (Figure 78)—deliciously fragrant,
colors from white through pink to red, and lavender shades. Select
either the tall single-stem type (called "column"), or the branching
type if you want many flowers on short stems. Blossoms are single or
double and may be recognized in the seedling stage if you prefer to
cull the single and grow only the double: double-blossom plants have
light green leaves, singles have dark green foliage. For January flowers,

sow seeds in August, though flowers may be had for Christmas if addi
tional light is supplied by 40- or 50-watt bulbs in reflectors. For cut
flowers through June, make successive sowings every other month
August through February. Plant only in sterilized soil to prevent root
rot, and watch temperature carefully—plants will grow "blind" (will not
set buds) if temperature gets up to 60 F. Space single-stem seedlings 3
inches apart in rows 6 inches apart; branching varieties require 6 inches
between plants and at least 8 inches between rows. Grow in full sun;
avoid wetting foliage. The column type may require support, as stems
often reach 3 feet in height and flower spikes are large and heavy.

MYOSOTIS sylvatica. FORGET-ME-NOT. 45–55 F

For masses of sky-blue short-stemmed flowers to give daintiness to
your arrangements, be sure to grow this old-time favorite, one of the
few true blues we have. For winter flowers sow seed in the bench
(germination 8 days) any time June through August; give plenty of

78. Trysomic Giant Imperial Stock (*Mathiola*). (GEORGE W. PARK SEED CO.
PHOTO)

79. *Nerine Bowdenii.*

moisture and keep in semishade. Thin to stand about 10 inches apart. If you prefer spring pot plants, sow in December and January; myosotis usually blooms in about 6 weeks. May also be propagated from summer cuttings. Recommended: *M. sylvatica alba,* pure white flowers; 'Blue Ball', sky-blue and free-flowering.

NEMESIA strumosa. 45–50 F

Delicate pansy-like flowers are borne profusely on stems about a foot high. In a cool greenhouse, blossoms remain for an exceptionally long period of time. Germination of seed takes 2 to 3 weeks at 55 F. Transplant seedlings to medium heavy soil in bench, space 8 inches apart, keep on dry side; pinch to induce branching. Seed sown in August will provide flowers from October through February, in white, pink, red, orange, or shades of blue. Recommended: 'Bluebird', large-flowering rare blue; 'Carnival', mixture of brilliant large flowers on compact plants.

NERINE sarniensis. GUERNSEY-LILY. 50 F

This tender bulb produces several brilliant spider-like blossoms atop a 1- to 2-foot spike which appears before foliage develops. Flowers are pink, crimson, or scarlet tinged with orange. They are not fussy as to soil, but require good drainage. Plant bulbs in summer, as many as 3 to a 5-inch pot, as root development is not extensive. Keep fairly dry at first—bulbs seems to prefer a rest period after growth starts in late

August—but give plenty of moisture during growth. Do not dry off until foliage yellows and matures in spring. Once established, roots do not like to be disturbed, so do not repot for several years; however, a top dressing of fresh soil in the fall is beneficial. While foliage is maturing, nerines like a monthly feeding with a complete fertilizer. *N. Bowdenii* (Figure 79) has bright rose-pink flowers.

ORCHID. *See Chapter 12.*

ORNITHOGALUM arabicum. ARABIAN STAR-OF-BETHLEHEM. **50–60 F**
Broad-petaled white blossoms with gleaming black centers (Figure 80) appear in clusters of 15 or more atop sturdy foot-high stems. Pot the tender bulbs in fall, keep cool and dark to promote root growth. When top growth appears, move to light and water well to induce spring flowering. After blooming, keep foliage growing until it ripens, dry off and store bulbs in pots until fall. Repot in fresh soil before new growth cycle begins. Other popular species for pot culture are *O. umbellatum* (Star-of-Bethlehem), green-margined white flowers; and *O. thyrsoides aureum* (chincherinchee, Figure 81), golden-yellow flowers.

80. *Ornithogalum arabicum.*

(GEORGE W. PARK SEED CO. PHOTO)

81. *Ornithogalum thyrsoides.*

(MERRY GARDENS PHOTO)

82. *Osmanthus fragrans.* (MERRY GARDENS PHOTO)

OSMANTHUS fragrans. SWEET-OLIVE. 45–55 F

Tiny white, extremely fragrant flowers nestle against dark green leaves of this delightful, decorative pot plant (Figure 82). Find a warm spot in the cool greenhouse—sweet-olive really prefers 55 F. Grows well in loam, clay, or garden soil, with some well-rotted manure and peatmoss added. Prefers diffused sunlight, so shade during summer. Keep soil moist but not water-soaked. Propagate by cuttings in June.

OXALIS. 45–60 F

Feathery foliage and numerous dainty blossoms of white, yellow, or shades of pink make oxalis (Color Plate II and Figure 83) a favorite basket plant. Plant the tender tubers (in early fall for winter flowering) in a mix of loam, humus, and coarse sand. Water thoroughly but allow to become moderately dry between waterings. Grow in full sun. Tubers rest during summer.

83. *Oxalis cernua.* (MERRY GARDENS PHOTO)

84. Passiflora. (GEORGE W. PARK SEED CO. PHOTO)

PASSIFLORA. PASSION-FLOWER.   **50–65 F**

One of the most prolific vines you can grow under glass; in fact, if not controlled it will run rampant throughout the greenhouse. Creeping tendrils penetrate the most unlikely places and you may discover, as I did, that it is growing not only inside the greenhouse but outside as well. In spite of this ambition, the exotic, intricately fashioned flowers (Figure 84) are so beautiful you can overlook its vigor. In limited space it can be restrained somewhat when grown as a pot plant. My vine was started from a cutting salvaged from the office wastebasket. It was rooted in sand and planted directly in the ground at the south end of my greenhouse, in garden soil containing a considerable quantity of coal ashes. Vines start easily from seeds or cuttings in early spring, and bloom continuously until well into cool weather. Blossoms resemble water-lilies supporting a crown of many filaments surrounding what appear to be three nails. Colors are white, delicate shades of lavender to dark purple, or dark red. When blooming stops, cut plant back to the ground or pot level. If pot-grown, remove and replace about half the soil without disturbing roots. Provide a support at the beginning; tendrils will find their own support as the vine grows. Flowers last only one day, so cut them early in the morning to enjoy them to their fullest.

PELARGONIUM. GERANIUM.   **45–55 F**

The great value of a geranium is that it blooms and blooms. Just a few pots bring constant color. If you collect geraniums, giving all or a good part of your greenhouse to them, what a picture you will have (Color Plate VI and Figures 42, 85–89). The flowers are handsomely diversified—red, rose, pink, salmon, lavender, blush, white, stippled, blended; single and double.

Zonals—green-leaved, fancy-leaved, dwarf

I have been referring only to the familiar green-leaved zonal type; do you know the fancy-leaved zonals? The varied hues of their foliage is almost as colorful as the big flowers of the plain-leaved zonals. They are fascinating to collect, especially if you select from rather definite categories, as gold-and-silver tricolors like 'Skies of Italy'; green-and-yellow bicolors or butterfly geraniums like 'Happy Thought'; yellow-and-brown class to which the delightful fairly dwarf 'Alpha' belongs; silver-leaveds like 'Wilhelm Langguth'; and gold-leaveds like 'Verona'. More than fifty different fancy-leaved geraniums are available.

Quite a collection of dwarf zonals, both the easy ones with plain leaves and the more challenging, often tiny and fancy-leaved kind, can be grown on one greenhouse shelf; they are showy because most of these small plants produce sizable flowers. 'Tu-Tone' is delectable pale pink, 'Prince Valiant' bright crimson; the pink-veined 'North Star' and 'Whitecap' are quite irresistible.

85. Dwarf zonal geranium 'Kleiner Liebling'. (MERRY GARDENS PHOTO)

Scented-leaved geraniums

Scented-leaved geraniums become giant shrubs in the greenhouse. One or two rose- or mint-scented types are very decorative and full of fragrance when the sun shines hard upon them, but they propagate so easily from cuttings that you can always have a few small plants coming along. There are many leaf forms and growth habits—maybe you would like to start with one in each category of scent: rose, mint, lemon, fruit, nut, spice, and pungent. Study a specialist's catalogue (like that of Merry Gardens, Camden, Maine) and you will go quite mad trying to select.

Ivy-leaved, regal, and oddities

Ivy-leaved geraniums make the loveliest possible basket plants by themselves or combined with other plants—begonias, ageratum, or trailing petunias. If winters are very dull and you do not have fluorescent lights, the ivy-leaved type may not bloom till late February, but then what a display from the lavender-blue 'Santa Paula', pink 'Comtesse de Grey', or 'The Blush' with flowers like little rosebuds.

When it comes to regal or Lady Washington pelargoniums, what a long and handsome spring display they give in the greenhouse! You can have a lovely time with even a few plants, perhaps the cerise 'Easter Greeting', pansy-type 'Madame Layal', pink 'Cover Girl', and brilliant 'Salmon Splendor'. You will certainly want more if your hobby is geraniums.

If you collect geraniums, in time you may also be attracted to geranium oddities, species like night-fragrant *P. gibbosum*, climbing *P. scandens*, or pretty, thorny, sweetheart geranium *P. echinatum*. What fascination lies in this group alone.

Culture and propagation

Geraniums are best suited to a cool greenhouse and a night temperature of 45 to 55 F. Good air circulation and a fresh atmosphere are essential. Contrary to popular belief, geraniums must be watered well. True, they do best when allowed to dry out between waterings, but mine are usually watered once a day in winter and twice a day in summer, depending on the weather. Through gray winter days, once or twice a week is sometimes enough. You have to *feel* the soil to know, for overwatering can be as harmful as dryness and subsequent wilting.

86. Trailing ivy-leaved geranium 'New Dawn'.
(MERRY GARDENS PHOTO)

87. Regal geranium 'Salmon Splendor'.
(MERRY GARDENS PHOTO)

88. Pansy-type geranium 'Earliana'.
(MERRY GARDENS PHOTO)

89. Cactus-flowered geranium 'Noel'.
(MERRY GARDENS PHOTO)

In winter, geraniums revel in full sun and prove it with a magnificent crop of flowers. In summer, shading is necessary to avoid burning of foliage and to prevent rapid drying out of soil, especially in small pots.

Actually, there is no part of a geranium that will not make a nice new plant if propagated in sand. I have stuck inch-long pieces into the propagating bed just on a whim, and found to my delight that they developed into fine little flowering plants in a short time.

How to make a tree geranium (Figure 90)

Very decorative for the greenhouse is a pair of tree or standard geraniums, especially well-trained double-flowered zonals. The glowing salmon 'Mrs. E. G. Hill', pink-and-white 'Apple Blossom Rosebud', pale pink 'Princess Fiat', or strong 'Olympic Red' make handsome standards in only a little over a year's time. Select straight healthy cuttings that have been rooted in February in sand, and plant each in a 2½-inch pot. Fertilize and train to a single stem by pinching off all side shoots. But don't pinch out the top for this causes branching that you do not want *yet*. Shift to larger pots as necessary until your plants are big enough for a final 8-inch pan. This could well be mid-September if you promote growth by regular fertilizing, say every other week.

When plants are 8 to 10 inches high, support them with 15-inch bamboo stakes. Fasten stems to stakes with plant ties. As stems reach 30 to 36 inches, pinch tops to induce branching and the formation of a flowering head. Blooming starts in March or April.

Handsome dozen

The big zonals are the best for long-time bloom—here are twelve to give you enormous satisfaction. (But for fun I hope you will investigate the other fascinating groups.) 'Birds Egg', 'Blaze', 'Double New Life', 'Enchantress', 'Helen Van Pelt Wilson', 'Magnificent', 'Merry Gardens White', 'Mrs. E. G. Hill', 'Orange Richard', 'Party Dress', 'Apple Blossom Rosebud', 'Toyon'.

PEPEROMIA.   60–65 F

Peperomias, mostly low and bushy, are grown for their decorative and variegated foliage—pale green, emerald, metallic, gray-green, olive, and bronzy; some leaves are heart-shaped, others pod-like—and are useful for edging benches or in hanging baskets if trailing varieties are

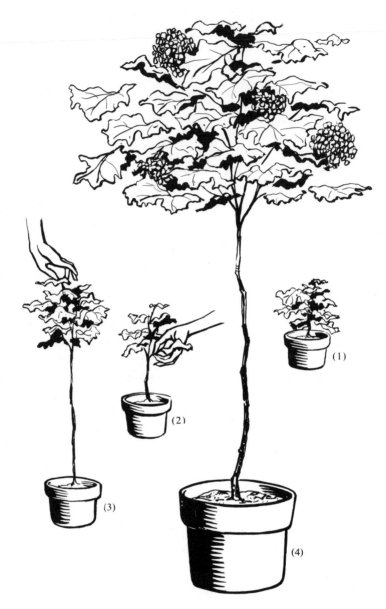

90. HOW TO MAKE A TREE GERANIUM. Select a sturdy plant with a straight main stem, remove all other stems and branches, continue to remove lower foliage as plant grows to desired height. Then pinch out the center to encourage the top to spread—and there you have a conversation piece for your garden under glass.

selected. They prefer an equal-fourths mix of garden soil, well-rotted manure, peat, and sand. Peperomias prefer to be grown on the dry side and should become moderately dry between waterings. Grow in filtered or diffused sunlight. Propagate from seeds which take about 20 days to germinate, or from cuttings.

PILEA. 60–65 F

A group of bushy plants extremely easy to cultivate under glass as they need the humid atmosphere of a greenhouse. Leaves are colorful, ranging from dark green through dark brown, some with silver. Potting mix should be rich in humus or organic matter with an all-purpose fertilizer added. Pilea prefers filtered or diffused sunlight; keep moist except when resting. Recommended: *P. cadierei* (aluminum-plant) and its dwarf form, *P. cadierei minima; P. microphylla* (artillery-plant), small, succulent fernlike foliage; *P. nummulariaefolia* (creeping-Charley), long trailing stems of puckered light-green leaves; *P. repens,* quilted coppery-brown leaves.

PITTOSPORUM Tobira. JAPANESE PITTOSPORUM. 40–55 F

This shrubby plant does well in a cool or an intermediate greenhouse; likes bright light or full sun, but can also be grown in diffused sunlight. Pot in equal parts garden soil, well-rotted manure, and peat or humus, with a little sand added for good drainage. Water thoroughly, then allow to dry somewhat before the next watering. Dark green leather-like leaves of *P. Tobira* have a lighter middle rib; *P. Tobira variegata* (Figure 91) has green and white leaves. Seeds germinate in about 15 days.

91. *Pittosporum Tobira variegata.* (MERRY GARDENS PHOTO)

PLUMBAGO capensis. LEADWORT.   **45–55 F**

Partially climbing or upright and straggling, *P. capensis* produces azure-blue flowers at the tip of every branch from spring to fall. *P. capensis alba* has white flowers.

POLIANTHES tuberosa. TUBEROSE.   **55–65 F**

Richly scented single or double waxy white flowers are easily cultivated under glass. Staggered plantings of tender tubers from January to May will furnish blossoms until late summer. A mix of 2 parts garden loam, 1 part peatmoss or leafmold, and 1 part sand should keep them growing well if given plenty of water after growth is evident. They like full sun. Carrying over to another season is not always satisfactory; you may prefer to buy new bulbs each year.

PRIMULA. PRIMROSE.   **45–50 F**

Two species of quite different flowering habit are the most popular for greenhouse culture. *P. malacoides* produces dainty flowers on fairly long stems almost continuously; *P. obconica* blossoms in huge clusters the size of a half-dollar. Plants bloom January to May. Colors range from white through pink to reds and lavender. Seed is extremely fine and best sown on moist sphagnum moss in a flat and enclosed in plastic. Sow *P. malacoides* April to August; *P. obconica* March to June. Remove plastic when seedlings appear; transplant to a mix of 1 part soil and 1 part sand in flats. Before seedlings crowd each other in the flat, transplant to 3-inch pots using the same mix. Make final shift to 4- or 5-inch pots before roots become potbound, using a mix of 2 parts soil, 1 part sand, 1 part well-rotted manure; or equal parts sand and soil with a complete fertilizer. Water freely, especially during summer; primroses wilt badly when moisture is insufficient. Shade is essential during summer. The foliage of *P. obconica* may cause severe skin irritation to some gardeners, so handle carefully, especially when transplanting.

RANUNCULUS.   **45–50 F**

Ranunculus produce double camellia-type blossoms of red, yellow, pink, or white. Culture and propagation are same as for anemone.

ROSA. ROSE.   **50–60 F**

Purchase plants of varieties suitable for indoor culture, including miniatures (Figure 92), or dig some from your garden in the fall. Pot in a mix of 3 parts garden loam and 1 part peatmoss or well-rotted manure, in pots large enough to take entire root system without squeezing and to allow for additional growth. Place on sides in cold-frame or protected area and cover with sufficient hay or straw to prevent freezing. In late December, bring into the greenhouse, place under the bench and syringe frequently to promote bud development; move up to the bench. Mulch with peatmoss to prevent drying out roots, but avoid overwatering. Fertilize periodically while in active growth. If you plan to grow them in the greenhouse for another year, plunge pots outdoors during summer. In early October, inspect carefully for insects and repot if necessary; otherwise, remove an inch of topsoil and replace with fresh soil. Place in coldframe and repeat cultural directions above. If pruning is necessary, do it just before placing in coldframe, or before the roses are brought into greenhouse for forcing. A 60 to 70 per cent humidity in the greenhouse and controlled ventilation are beneficial. Spring cuttings root in about 2 months with bottom heat of 70 F. Pot in 2½-inch pots and shift to larger pots as necessary. Dust roses with sulfur to eliminate mildew. Red spider and aphids may attack roses.

SAINTPAULIA. AFRICAN-VIOLET.   60–70 F

African-violets (Color Plate II) must be grown warm and moist and given a relative humidity of 50 per cent. Light has special significance

92. Miniature rose 'Oakington Ruby'. (MERRY GARDENS PHOTO)

in their culture—for strong, healthy foliage and a profusion of continuous blooms, plenty of light but no direct sunlight is essential. If light intensity is too great, tight growth and bleached or burned foliage will be noticeable. If light is insufficient, plants tend to be leggy and produce fewer flowers. Flowering African-violets can be produced from seed in 6 to 7 months, or from leaf cuttings in 8 or 9 months. Seed does not always reproduce true, however, so to assure duplication of a certain variety, propagate from leaves (Chapter 14).

Pot in a mix of sterilized soil, sand, peatmoss, and well-rotted manure, or in a commercial African-violet mix. Water from top or bottom, but avoid splashing water on foliage and thus avoid leaf-spot. Use tepid water if possible. Complete liquid fertilizer should be applied every 3 to 4 weeks, in diluted strength to avoid burning delicate roots. As an added precaution, never apply fertilizer to dry soil. Avoid drafts; African-violets do not like sudden changes in temperature. They seem to adapt themselves to one particular location and grow best when left undisturbed except for an occasional turning of the plant to assure even distribution of light and balanced, symmetrical development of foliage. If you grow many African-violets, you must be constantly on the watch for pests and diseases that could raise havoc with your entire collection: mildew, crown rot, nematodes, mealy bugs, and cyclamen mites. Descriptions and controls are given in Chapter 6.

SAXIFRAGA sarmentosa. STRAWBERRY-BEGONIA. 45–55 F

Leaves of this vine are dark and round with silvery veins. Numerous runners produce plantlets that hang over the side of pot or basket. Prefers filtered or diffused sunlight and equal-thirds mix of loam, well-rotted manure, and peat or humus—with sand for drainage. Water thoroughly, then allow to dry moderately before rewatering. Propagate by rooting the plantlets.

SCHIZANTHUS. POOR-MAN'S-ORCHID; BUTTERFLY-FLOWER. 45–50 F

Newer strains produce blossoms as large as 2 inches across, literally smothering the foliage in brilliant color; others have more subtly tinted flowers resembling orchid blossoms; they are desirable as cut flowers as well as pot plants. Foliage is lacy or fernlike; plants grow 2 feet high except the dwarf varieties. Sow seeds in August for March or April bloom, in January for late-spring flowers. Sow on and cover seeds ⅛ inch with milled sphagnum. Seeds germinate quickly; if you

93. Schizanthus mixture. (GEORGE W. PARK SEED CO. PHOTO)

enclose in plastic, inspect daily for germination and remove plastic to prevent leggy seedlings. Seedlings grow rapidly and are ready to transplant in a very short time. Grow as bench or pot plants or in deep flats, depending upon whether you want long or short stems. Space bench plants about 8 inches apart—these will grow to long stems. If planted in seed flats, space 3 inches apart and allow to grow to a single stem; these will be shorter-stemmed than those in benches. If you prefer pot plants, shift seedlings to 2½-inch pots, then to larger pots as necessary. Plants should not be allowed to become potbound until they have been transplanted into their final pots. Pinch several times to secure full bushy plants. Soil mix should be 1 part each garden loam and leafmold with some well-rotted manure added. For early flowering, give approximately 4 hours of additional light daily starting at sundown. Remember, however, that other plants in the greenhouse may be adversely affected by additional light. Recommended: Dr. Badger's Hybrids, the best-known strain of mixed colors; Monarch Hybrids, a strain of dwarf plants with large flowers in many colors.

SENECIO cruentus. CINERARIA.   **45–50 F**

Bright colored free-blooming pot plants with daisylike blossoms in pink, rose, blue to dark purple shades (Color Plate I). Sow seeds in June for January bloom; in September for spring flowers. Sow on moist sphagnum and take care that it does not dry out during germination: Transplant seedlings to flats, then to 2½- or 3-inch pots, in light soil or a mix of 3 parts soil and 1 part well-rotted manure. Shift to 5-inch pots, where plants will bloom about 4 weeks after they become potbound. Fertilize biweekly. Through summer, keep plants out of direct sun and water frequently to prevent wilting. Discard plants when flowering is finished. Recommended: Palette, a strain of dwarf plants with 3-inch blossoms in brilliant and delicate colors; Hansa, small foliage, large early-blooming scarlet, red, crimson, pink, and blue flowers.

SINNINGIA speciosa. GLOXINIA.   **60–70 F**

Large trumpet-shaped blossoms of this gesneriad are of velvety texture, so beautiful they defy description (Color Plate I). Hybrids are available in just about every color except yellow.

For your first gloxinias, purchase tubers from a gesneriad specialist or your garden center. Plant one tuber to a 5- or 6-inch pot, the concave (indented) side of the tuber up. Cover tuber with about ¾ inch of potting medium which must be fibrous, loose, well-aerated, and quick draining. Gentle bottom heat is helpful in starting growth, but not essential. Pots can be placed in any convenient warm spot, but as soon as growth appears above soil, move to good light but not direct sun. Growth will now be rapid; all shoots except the main one should be rubbed off as they appear—a gloxinia should always be grown with a single crown if you want a handsome plant that produces flowers superior in quality and quantity. (However, you can let the secondary shoots grow to about 2 inches, gently pull them from the tuber and place them in a propagating case to root.)

Fertilize growing gloxinias every 10 days with a complete houseplant fertilizer, keep evenly moist but never soggy, and try to provide relative humidity of 50 to 60 per cent. After flowering, keep foliage growing until it yellows and dies back, indicating that the tuber has become dormant. Twist off dead foliage and water soil occasionally, just enough to keep tuber from shriveling. A new growing cycle may start in a few weeks, or the tuber may rest for three months—just watch for new growth, then repeat cultural instructions above.

Gloxinias grow very easily from dustlike seeds. Sow on top of moist milled sphagnum moss, mist lightly with warm water to anchor seeds to moss. Enclose container in plastic and give it bottom heat and light (but not direct sun). Germination takes 10 to 30 days—the fresher the seed the faster it germinates. For a specimen plant with abundant flowers, transplant the seedling directly to a 5- or 6-inch pot, where it will flower in 6 to 8 months. For earlier but smaller and sparser flowers, transplant seedlings to 3-inch pots. (Caution: the tuber starts to form underground as soon as germination occurs—be careful in transplanting seedlings not to separate the tiny tuber from the top growth.) Culture for seedlings from this point is same as for tubers. Gloxinias are also easily propagated from leaf cuttings.

STREPTOSOLEN Jamesonii.   50–60 F

Formerly known as *Browallia Jamesonii,* and still popularly called "orange browallia," this shrubby vine with small green leaves and orange-red blooms needs a warm spot in your 50 F greenhouse, good air circulation, and plenty of light but not direct sunlight. Grow in equal-thirds mix of soil, well-rotted manure, peat, with a little sand added for drainage if your soil is heavy. Cuttings propagated early in summer will be ready to bench (space them 8 inches apart) or pot in July. Blossoms appear in January; vine continues to flower for several weeks. Keep evenly moist but do not overwater. Taper off on water when plant is resting after blooming.

TRACHELOSPERMUM jasminoides. STAR-JASMINE.   45–50 F

A delightful climber with glossy green foliage and cluster blossoms of fragrant star-shaped flowers from early spring well into fall (Figure 94), and an ideal plant for the cool greenhouse. Restrain lush growth by snipping to desired size; support vine on a trellis. If blooming stops during normal flowering period, withhold water for a week or two; a semi-dormant state seems to encourage flowering. Requires little special care; can be grown in the same pot for several years. *T. asiaticum* (yellow star-jasmine) has yellowish-white flowers from late January to autumn.

TRACHYMENE caerulea. BLUE LACE-FLOWER.   45–50 F

Delicate lacy flat sky-blue flowers lend a pleasing airiness to floral arrangements and provide one of the few touches of blue available in

94. *Trachelospermum jasminoides.* (MERRY GARDENS PHOTO)

the garden under glass; it is particularly attractive with pink carnations. If you want only a few plants, sow seed directly in 4- or 5-inch pots, or for a plentiful supply, plant directly in bench; seedlings do not transplant well and are set back when shifted. Use light soil and have good drainage—water-logged soil may stunt growth. Seedlings in the bench should be thinned to 6 inches apart in rows about 10 inches apart. Seed sown in June will flower at Christmas, in August by February. Responds to additional light, and flowers may be had 4 to 5 weeks earlier if extra light is given. This plant was formerly known as *Didiscus caerulea* and some dealers still list it under the old name.

TRADESCANTIA. SPIDERWORT; INCH-PLANT.   **50–55 F**

Fast-growing trailing plants in a variety of foliage colors: pale green and white tinted with purple, green and cream, coppery green with purple underside, even gold. Flowers may be white, lavender pink, or dark purple. Prefers ample air circulation, good light or diffused sunlight, soil mix of equal parts garden loam, well-rotted manure, peat, and sand. Water well, but allow to become moderately dry between waterings. Cuttings root easily in sand.

TRITONIA crocosmaeflora. 45–50 F

Colorful orange-crimson cup-shaped blossoms of this easily handled corm can be cut for bouquets. In October, plant several of the small corms in a bulb-pan in 3 parts soil, 1 part peatmoss, 1 part sand, pressing them in gently. Water thoroughly and place pots under the bench until top growth is evident. Bring up to benches and increase water; keep moist but not wet and they will flower in April. They like plenty of fresh air and sunlight, although some shading may be necessary during summer. Gradually reduce watering after flowering to allow foliage to die back naturally. Dry off corms and hold for next season. *T. crocosmaeflora aurantiaca* has deep orange flowers.

TROPAEOLUM majus. NASTURTIUM. 45–50 F

For attractive foliage and long-stemmed fragrant flowers, try some old-fashioned nasturtiums. They are ideal for edging benches, and excellent to cut for flower arrangements. Flower colors include rich golden yellow, light cream, dark mahogany, scarlet, and cerise. Buy a carefully blended mixture of seeds for a brilliant display. Soil should be light: garden loam and sand. If soil is too rich in organic matter, foliage will be luxuriant with few flowers. Do not use high-nitrogen fertilizer. Nasturtiums like to be grown in full sun and are quick to bloom. Soak the seeds overnight before planting, to speed germination. Foliage is often used as a salad green. Recommended: 'Golden Gleam', rich golden yellow; 'Mahogany Gleam', deep mahogany red; 'Moon Gleam', light golden cream.

TULBAGHIA cepacea. 45–50 F

Evergreen foliage with almost year-round, extremely fragrant lavender-pink blossoms (you may know the plant under its old name of *T. fragrans*). Pot any time in a well-drained soil mix. Keep in semi-shade during summer; give full sun rest of year. Keep moderately moist. The foliage of *T. violacea* (Color Plate II) has a pungent onion odor if injured.

VALLOTA speciosa. SCARBOROUGH-LILY. 50–55 F

Clusters of 2-inch scarlet lilylike flowers (Figure 95) appear in spring and summer if liquid fertilizer is given every 3 to 4 weeks during active growth. Pot the tender bulbs in fall in well-drained fibrous soil; never

95. *Vallota speciosa.*

allow the soil to dry out, but keep moderately moist even during rest period following flowering. Disturb roots as little as possible, repotting only when pot is overcrowded.

VELTHEIMIA viridifolia. 45–55 F

A sun-loving plant with sword-shaped leaves and clusters of drooping red-tinged yellow blossoms that is at its best in spring if bulbs are planted in November. Use a pot 2 inches larger than the bulb, and a mix of garden loam, peatmoss or leafmold, and sand. Water thoroughly, then hold back on water until top growth is evident. Increase moisture and keep well watered until flowering ceases and foliage dies back. Dry off completely. In September or October, repot or scrape off the top inch or two of soil and replace with fresh soil; start into growth again. Feed every 4 to 6 weeks with liquid fertilizer.

ZANTEDESCHIA. CALLA-LILY. 55–65 F

This old-time garden favorite has been modernized and is available in glorious shades of apricot, pink, red, yellow, gold, and cream. It can be brought into bloom almost any time of year in the greenhouse, though winter bloom is probably the most appreciated. Rhizomes are started in a mixture of peatmoss and sand. When established, pot in a mix of soil, peat, and well-rotted manure, with sand added for good drainage since they like plenty of water when in full growth. When growth is well established, feed once or twice with a complete liquid fertilizer. If planted in August for winter bloom, give plenty of light and good air circulation. Shade from June to planting time. After flowering, rest by withholding moisture. Recommended: *Z. aethiopica,* pure white velvety textured blooms and waxy arrow-shaped leaves; *Z. Rehmannii,* dwarf plant with lovely large light pink flowers; Sunrise Hybrids, a strain of colors from apricot through yellow, gold, cream, and pink to red; *Z. Childsiana* (Figure 96).

96. *Zantedeschia Childsiana.* (MERRY GARDENS PHOTO)

ZYGOCACTUS truncatus. CHRISTMAS CACTUS.   **55–60 F**

Flat, green, pendent branches drip with double-skirted ballerina-like flowers of white through rose and orange-pink to brighten the greenhouse during the Christmas season. Requires well-drained soil of equal parts leafmold, peatmoss, garden loam, and clean sharp sand. Keep in full sun and water regularly through spring. A cool location and a drying-off period through summer are absolutely necessary to assure blooms. I achieve best results by placing plants under the bench during summer, watering seldom until mid-October when I bring them up into the light and warmth of the greenhouse and increase watering. Feeding with liquid manure every 2 weeks once active growth starts is beneficial, but this should be discontinued when buds develop. When blooming period is over, you will see that the plant has expended itself to the point of appearing shriveled. Give plenty of water and its normal fleshy appearance will be restored. Cuttings taken in September (they root easily in moist sand) make 4-inch flowering plants in about 15 months. Repot mature plants in spring after flowering only every third or fourth year. Although the recommended temperature is 60 F, I have exceptionally good results on shelves in my 52 F greenhouse.

Part Four

Useful Lists
and Guides

The Greenhouse Garden
Month by Month

No two months of greenhouse gardening are quite the same. With a wealth of plant material to select from, and with your individual gardening program to develop, each month will be excitingly different. A great deal of the planting and manual work occurs during two months: September, when you start winter-flowering seeds and bulbs; January, when you prepare for spring. The beauty, fragrance, and excitement of the other ten months more than compensate for the extra activity in September and January.

For your consideration when planning your schedule, here is a month-by-month list of greenhouse activities, and a list of plants that can be in flower each month. Probably you will not select everything listed for a given month, but you will see that it is possible, with a little planning, to have flowers in your greenhouse every month of the year.

JANUARY

Things to do

Remove ice that forms around automatic ventilators; keep snow away from exterior portions of heater or vents that extend through the greenhouse wall. Go easy on watering of plants, especially on dark stormy days.

Start seeds of African-violets, beets for late winter harvest, begonias, browallia, calendula, carrots for spring, felicia, gloxinia, gypsophila, impatiens, kalanchoe, lobelia, nierembergia, petunia, salpiglossis, schizanthus, snapdragon, sweet-alyssum, sweet-pea, tomatoes for spring, trachymene.

Start cuttings of African-violet, ageratum, beloperone, browallia, campanula, carnation, clerodendrum, crassula, crossandra, gardenia, geranium.

Pot begonia, caladium, calla-lily, and gloxinia tubers; amaryllis bulbs.

Start bringing in potted tulips, daffodils, and hyacinths to force.

In flower

Abutilon, acalypha, African-violet, amaryllis, anemone, ardisia, azalea, begonia, beloperone, bougainvillea, bouvardia, browallia, cacti, calendula, camellia, chrysanthemum, cineraria, crocus, crossandra, crown-of-thorns, cyclamen, daffodil, felicia, freesia, gardenia, geranium, gloxinia, gypsophila, heliotrope, hyacinth, impatiens, iris (Dutch), kalanchoe, lachenalia, lantana, myosotis, narcissus, nasturtium, orchids (cattleya, cymbidium, oncidium), osmanthus, oxalis, poinsettia, *Primula malacoides,* rose, snapdragon, stock, sweet-pea, tulip.

FEBRUARY

Things to do

Provide adequate air circulation to maintain a healthy atmosphere during dull winter weather. Have some fun. Sow seeds of a few annuals and keep records of germination time to compare with later sowings when days are longer and brighter.

Start seeds of marigolds and stocks for May bloom.

Pot rhizomes of achimenes for flowers in 8 to 10 weeks.

Bring in fall-potted crocus for bloom in 6 weeks; also additional pots of tulips, daffodils, and hyacinths.

Buy seeds, flats, pots, planting medium, for bedding plants and annuals for your outdoor garden.

In flower

Amaryllis, anemone, calendula, camellia, cineraria, daffodil, felicia, freesia, hyacinth, lachenalia, myosotis, nasturtium, orchids, *Primula malacoides,* ranunculus, snapdragon, sweet-alyssum, trachymene, tulip.

MARCH

Things to do

Adjust feeding and watering schedule for actively growing plants. Cut forsythia branches from outdoor bushes and force into bloom in the greenhouse. Try your hand at making corsages from your cymbidium orchids—it's easier than you think. Buy the little vials, green floral tape, fine wire, and colorful ribbon from your florist. You may proudly wear your very own corsage on Easter Day!

Start seeds of cucumbers at 60 F for early summer harvest; petunias, snapdragons, and ageratum for the outdoor garden.

In flower

Amaryllis, begonia, browallia, felicia, geranium, gypsophila, lobelia, orchids (cymbidium and dendrobium), *Primula obconica,* star-jasmine, sweet-pea, trachymene.

APRIL

Things to do

Shade the entire roof area of your greenhouse by the end of April, especially if you are growing orchids; the sun's warmth is increasing. Repot, as necessary, pot plants that have finished flowering; also divide and repot orchids before new leads extend themselves. If your vent thermostat was set high for winter weather, reset it at ten degrees above the heat thermostat setting.

Prepare bulb list for next winter's forcing and place your bulb order early.

Bench cucumbers started from seed in March; make chrysanthemum cuttings; start seeds of calendula, marigold, gypsophila, and morning-glory for the outdoor garden.

In flower

Agapanthus, azalea, chrysanthemum (annual), crinum, gardenia, geranium, stock, sweet-pea, ranunculus.

MAY

Things to do

If you live in an extremely sunny area, full greenhouse shade may be necessary this month. Decide now whether you will keep your plants in the greenhouse during summer months; if not, select outdoor locations now to facilitate transfer of plants next month. If weather turns warm, it may be necessary to hose down greenhouse walks and spray-mist the foliage now.

Purchase or make your own chrysanthemum cuttings for fall blooms. Pot bulbs of *Lilium auratum,* the goldband lily, for August flowering.

In flower

Calceolaria, calendula, chrysanthemum (annual), crinum, felicia, gardenia, Madonna lily, nasturtium, snapdragon, stock, sweet-pea.

JUNE

Things to do

Shade entire greenhouse if it is to be used during summer. Hose down walks and mist plants to lower the temperature and provide humidity. If general housecleaning is in order, move all plants outdoors by the end of the month before weather gets too warm to work in comfort; follow housecleaning suggestions on page 76. Plan your fall and winter growing schedule. Check supplies and order what you will need.

Start seeds of tomatoes for a September crop, snapdragons for winter bloom, and trachymene for Christmas flowering. Make cuttings of outdoor shrubs. Pot bulbs of *Lilium tigrinum,* tiger lily, for October bloom. Move camellias outdoors.

Then—enjoy the summer!

JULY

Things to do

Not much activity in the greenhouse this month. Hose walks and mist the air and plants for humidity. Make final pinch on most varieties of fall chrysanthemums by July 15. Sow seeds of snapdragons for winter bloom. Pot bulbs of *Lilium speciosum rubrum,* showy Japanese lily, for Christmas bloom.

Take a vacation, but get a sitter for the summer crops.

In flower

Begonia (wax and tuberous), bouvardia, chrysanthemum (annual), clerodendrum, gloxinia, star-jasmine.

AUGUST

Things to do

Change bench soil; or add sand, peatmoss or shredded osmunda fiber, and superphosphate or a 5-10-5 fertilizer (a 3-inch potful to a bushel of soil) to your present bench soil. Turn soil to distribute added material evenly. Let stand before using; it will be ready for a new crop when the gardening season starts in September.

Have heating system checked and serviced if this was not done during your general summer housecleaning.

Make geranium cuttings.

Start seeds of stocks for January bloom, trachymene for March flowers, and cyclamen for flowers in 15 to 18 months.

Pot freesia corms; also bulbs of Madonna lily for bloom next May.

In flower

Begonia (tuberous), bouvardia, gloxinia, *Lilium auratum,* passiflora, star-jasmine.

SEPTEMBER

Things to do

Return camellias to the greenhouse from their summer outdoors. Dig outdoor geraniums you wish to use as stock plants for cuttings; plant them under the edge of the greenhouse bench—they will add color while growing for future cutting.

Remove greenhouse shading by the end of the month. Be sure you have sufficient potting soil on hand to last through the winter. Start the heating system—there will be a few cool nights from now on. Provide yourself with enough pots, broken crock, and bonemeal to take care of bulb potting next month.

Pot anemone corms for January flowering. Start seeds of annual chrysanthemums, cauliflower for December use, snapdragons for January bloom, and sweet-peas for December flowering.

In flower

Begonias (tuberous), bouvardia, gloxinia, nerine.

OCTOBER

Things to do

Heat will be needed full time now, so adjust your watering schedule because plants dry out more quickly with the extra heat. Provide adequate air circulation around plants.

Pot hardy bulbs for winter forcing; store as explained in Chapter 11. Pot ranunculus corms. Sow seeds of calendula for late winter bloom. Take fuchsia cuttings. Move the Christmas cactus up to the bench from underneath, and increase watering it.

In flower

Begonias (tuberous), bouvardia, *Lilium tigrinum*, nemesia, nerine, orchids (epidendrum).

NOVEMBER

Things to do

Inspect stored bulbs to be sure they don't freeze. Cultivate bench soil to provide oxygen to roots of benched crops. Adjust watering schedule to winter weather. Cut chrysanthemums for your Thanksgiving table.

Make cuttings of carnations, Rex begonias, and evergreens. Sow seeds of stocks and snapdragons for April bloom. Pot bulbs of amaryllis, crinum, and veltheimia; and calla-lily rhizomes.

In flower

Calendula, chrysanthemums, crown-of-thorns, nemesia, nerine, snapdragons.

DECEMBER

Things to do

Put up wiring frame supports for carnation cuttings made in

November and December. Spray chrysanthemums against aphids. Cultivate bench soil.

Make cuttings of carnations, African-violets, and begonias. Bring in some potted bulbs for forcing.

Schedule as little work as possible. This is the season to enjoy your greenhouse efforts. The house is a riot of color for Christmas: red and white poinsettias, white and pink cyclamen, orange-red blossoms of crown-of-thorns, pendulous blossoms of Christmas cactus in profusion. Hanging baskets of browallia and oxalis are at their loveliest. Fragrance is everywhere from bouvardia, hyacinths, gardenias, and carnations.

Have a holiday party—share your fragrant and colorful blossoms with your friends and neighbors.

In flower

Ardisia, bouvardia, camellia, Christmas cactus, crown-of-thorns, cyclamen, freesia, *Lilium speciosum rubrum*, nasturtium, orchids (cattleyas and cymbidiums), poinsettias, snapdragons, sweet-peas, trachymene.

Plants suggested for various temperature ranges

40–45 F. Acuba.

40–50 F. Acacia, camellia.

40–55 F. Pittosporum.

45–50 F. Ageratum, albuca, anemone, calceolaria, calendula, dianthus, eschscholzia, fuchsia, gypsophila, hedera, lachenalia, lobularia, mathiola, nemesia, primula, ranunculus, schizanthus, senecio, trachelospermum, trachymene, tritonia, tropaeolum, tulbaghia.

45–55 F. Abutilon, agapanthus, antirrhinum, campanula, cyclamen, myosotis, osmanthus, pelargonium, plumbago, saxifraga, veltheimia.

45–60 F. Chrysanthemum, oxalis.

45–65 F. Azalea.

45–70 F. Dahlia, ferns.

50–55 F. Beloperone, brunsfelsia, ceropegia, chlorophytum, freesia, lobelia, nerine, tradescantia, vallota.

50–60 F. Acanthus, alstroemeria, araucaria, browallia, carissa, felicia, gladiolus, haemanthus, lilium, ornithogalum, rosa, streptosolen.

50–65 F. Clivia, passiflora.

50–70 F. Coleus, kalanchoe.

55–60 F. Allophyton, begonia (winter-flowering tuberous), hymenocallis, iris, manettia, zygocactus.

55–65 F. Acalypha, aeschynanthus, amarcrinum, aphelandra, ardisia, bouvardia, crinum, *Euphorbia splendens*, gloriosa, heliotropium, hippeastrum, impatiens, polianthes, zantedeschia.

55–70 F. Begonia (fibrous-rooted: wax, angelwing, cane-stemmed, small-leaved branching, hirsute), crossandra.

60–65 F. Achimenes, agloanema, alsophila, alternanthera, amomum, begonia (summer-flowering tuberous, pendent tuberous), bougainvillea, *Euphorbia pulcherrima*, gesneriads, gynura, peperomia, pilea.

60–70 F. Allamanda, begonia (rhizomatous), bromeliads, cacti and succulents, caladium, clerodendrum, saintpaulia, sinningia.

60–75 F. Codiaeum

65–70 F. Alocasia, anthurium, eucharis, gardenia.

Index